SINDONE

The Divine Remedy

by
Laura Clark

WGAW No. 997015
Copyright © 2009 Laura Clark
First Copyright 2004
All rights reserved.

ISBN: 978-0-9789499-4-5

LIBRARY OF CONGRESS CONTROL NUMBER: 2009912408

Published by Cradle Press

Cover painting and design by Laura Clark

Cover layout by Just Ink

Disclaimer: Sindone, The Divine Remedy is a fictional story with fictional characters. It is not intended maliciously.

PREFACE

SINDONE
(Pronunciation: sin' doe nay) From the Greek/Latin word, *Sindon*, meaning shroud or piece of sheet that can be made for a specific purpose.

In April-May of 2010 the Shroud of Turin, known in Italy as the Sindone, will be exhibited at the Turin Cathedral of Saint John the Baptist (in Turin, Italy). The Sindone has endured centuries of speculations, theories, experiments, and controversies. This story is not intended to provoke further controversy, though its subject matter may well lead us there; controversy seems to be the underlying impetus with everything pertaining to the Shroud of Turin.

In 1997 the premise of this story crept into me and nested. I was compelled to travel to Turin and subsequently research and write a story that would not loosen its grip on me until it materialized on paper in 2004. Then, as quickly and intensely as it motivated me, it quieted itself and took a nap in my bookcase for five years.

I saw the story as a movie, thus I wrote it as a screenplay. During its five year slumber, I would occasionally tell myself I should give it a rewrite and try to have it made into a movie. One night in 2009, I pulled it off the shelf and read it again. I knew immediately that *this* story was the only story I wanted to communicate.

This story is fiction. Though rooted in research, it is intended solely as an exploration of the relationships between suffering and salvation, doubt and faith, science and religion, mankind and Christ.

I decided to publish the story as a book, but retain the screenplay format. Screenplays are great fun and very easy to read. They are quick in pacing and full of dialogue and action as they unravel inside the integrity of the three act structure. The reader is able to use his/her imagination to fill in the descriptive gaps and to visualize the characters and settings.

Screenplay jargon is unfamiliar to most readers, thus I have departed from using abbreviated "cues" and instead have written them in their entirety. I do, however, suggest reading this short list before you turn out the lights and begin watching the movie, so to speak.

Decoding Screenplay Terminology:

INT. = Interior scene location

EXT. = Exterior scene location

I/E. = Interior and Exterior scene locations

(beat) = A short pause

TITLE = Text appearing on the screen (usually to indicate the year/location, e.g. Turin, Italy 2008)

CONTINUOUS = Multiple scenes occurring at the same time

Sound effects are always in UPPER CASE FONT

Characters are named in UPPER CASE FONT only when first introduced into the story

This story is dedicated to...

The memory of my father. His relationship to God was private, devoted, and withstood the trials and treasures of life.

My mother, whose love of travel, history, and the Bible inspired me to look deeper into the Sindone, travel to Turin, and fortify this story with research.

And to the true love story and adventures of

Remi & duBois...

SINDONE

The Divine Remedy

FADE IN:

I/E. DWELLING/GARDEN IN JERUSALEM -- CIRCA 29 A.D. --DAWN

MARY MAGDALENE runs down a dirt path panicked. She arrives at a small dwelling, enters and finds SIMON PETER sleeping. She shakes him.

                MARY MAGDALENE
         (out of breath)
      They have taken the Lord out of his
      tomb and we do not know where they
      have laid him.

Simon Peter and another DISCIPLE rouse themselves and the three run at full speed towards the tomb where Jesus was buried. They arrive at an empty tomb, the large round stone door rolled aside.

Simon Peter peers inside, then enters with trepidation. He stands before the stone slab and stares down at the burial wrapping and the napkin folded neatly next to it. He gently places his hand on the wrapping, and looks up towards heaven.

EXT. CEMETERY -- MORNING

TITLE: TURIN, ITALY ~ DECEMBER, 2008

FATHER GIOVANNI stands before a SMALL CROWD, RECITING THE TWENTY-THIRD PSALM IN ITALIAN. When he finishes, STELLA FORBES, a formidable woman of 64, takes a handful of dirt, tosses it into the grave, brushes her hands clean and turns to go, signaling LORENZO BOTARI, handsome and refined at 65, to meet her at the gazebo. He pulls the arm of AUGUST PARKER, an amiable man of 70, and they walk over to the gazebo, where Stella stands smoking a cigarette.

                STELLA
         (Agitated)
      He would have hated this funeral.
      Fat pig; I can't believe he gave
      himself a heart attack.

                LORENZO
      Stella, darling, be kind. Vincenze
      was your husband, remember?

                STELLA
      Of course I remember! Unlike you,
      Lorenzo, I kept track of my spouse.

STELLA (CONT'D)
Which leads me to the point of this little meeting: I am going public with the information. I am extending the courtesy of letting you know, but I don't want any arguments. Not today.

AUGUST
Stella, you are upset. Let's discuss this. You can't just--

STELLA
I can and bloody well will. Our work was monumental and we all deserve credit. Besides, it is time for the world to receive the gift Viviano left them. I will arrange a press conference. You are either with me or you're on your own.

LORENZO
I agree, we deserve to be recognized in our fields, but you realize we risk going to prison? Stella, I know you are upset with how the investigation is going.

STELLA
We have been at a dead end for five years now! Our only prayer of finding them is to expose the truth.

AUGUST
And when we do, Stella? What then?

STELLA
I don't know exactly, but I am tired of waiting. Vincenze's greatest regret was not knowing the results of the experiment. I want to do this for him, in his memory. Besides, have you looked at a calender? We are right on schedule with our original plan. The timing couldn't be more appropriate.

LORENZO
And what about the Vatican?

                    STELLA
          That is precisely why I want to
          take the upper hand with the press
          conference. I will call you with
          the details.

(in the background) Father Giovanni is sitting in his car
with the window down, eavesdropping. Upon hearing mention of
the Vatican, he dials his cell phone.

INT. JES ADLER'S DINING ROOM -- NIGHT

TITLE: POINT REYES, CALIFORNIA

JES ADLER, magnetic and unassuming, is celebrating his 30th
birthday with a dinner party. He is ruggedly handsome, with
shoulder length sandy brown hair and deep chestnut eyes.
Attending the party are his loving parents, JOE and BEV
ADLER, both in their early seventies; the distinguished
PROFESSOR BARROWS, 63; Jes' neighbor, the elderly, quirky
PRETTY JANE THOMPSON; and his best friends JOHN and BECCA
PORTER, both in their late twenties. The group is SINGING a
rowdy rendition of "HAPPY BIRTHDAY" as Bev carries in the
cake, alight with thirty candles. The table is filled with
opened gifts, dinner remnants and empty bottles of wine. Jes
cuts into the cake as his golden retriever, SUNDANCE, waits
for a handout.

                    BECCA
               (rubbing her large
                pregnant belly)
          Oh, My God, I hope it's chocolate.
          Please tell me there is some
          chocolate in there!

                    JOHN
          Look out, buddy, you'll be lucky to
          taste that cake with this one
          around.

                    JES
          So who is the chocoholic, you or
          the baby?

                    BECCA
               (diving into her cake)
          Oh, the baby. But don't you know
          that motherhood is all about
          sacrifice? Bev, back me up on this.

                    JOHN
          Isn't she beautiful. Man can you
          believe I'm gonna be a daddy soon?

                    JES
          Hey, have you figured out what to
          do on the Coleman job yet? I've got
          most of their windows ready, so I
          can handle the install while you
          are away changing diapers.

                    JOHN
          Listen to this guy, talking about
          work on his birthday. Man you are
          in serious need of a life!

EXT. JES' FRONT YARD -- LATER

They wrap up their evening and Jes sees them off. Professor
Barrows escorts Pretty Jane to her home next door. Becca
waddles her way down the path and into the car with John's
help. They bid Jes GOOD NIGHT and HAPPY BIRTHDAY.

INT. JES' LIVING ROOM -- CONTINUOUS

Bev sees Jes coming back into the house. She stops washing
the dishes and signals Joe to get Jes to sit down. She enters
nervously and presents Jes with a small, worn envelope.

                    BEV
          This is for you today, sweetheart.

Jes opens the envelope and finds a note and a gold medal on a
chain. He admires the medal with the face of Christ on it and
some words in Latin, then READS the note ALOUD.

                    JES
          "For my son, on his thirtieth
          birthday. May the Holy Face of
          Christ protect you always. I love
          you every moment, no matter how far
          away the Lord may have taken me.
          Maria"

                    BEV
          (beat) I have been tempted to give
          this to you so many times... but I
          resisted, wanting to respect her
          wish that you receive it today. It
          was the least I could do...

                    BEV(CONT'D)
          she gave us the greatest gift of
          our lives, son.

                    JOE
          If this makes you change your mind
          about wanting to find her, you know
          we are willing to help you, Jes.

                    JES
          No, I haven't changed my mind. But
          this...

                    BEV
          I know it must be a shock to you.
          It's her only communication to you
          in your entire life. I don't know
          why she wanted to wait until you
          were thirty to get it, but many
          things about your birth mother are
          a mystery.

                    JES
          Listen, I'm really tired. Can we
          talk about this later?

                    JOE
          Of course. Come on, Bev. We've got
          a long drive anyway. Good night,
          son. And happy birthday.

Bev and Joe hug and kiss Jes and depart. Jes sits staring at
the medal and trying to read the inscription. He rereads the
note to himself and then unlatches the chain, puts on the
medal, and looks at himself in the mirror. Light from above
refracts off the medal and onto Jes' reflection in the
mirror, causing him to squint.

EXT. JES' DRIVEWAY -- MORNING

JES is collecting tools and lumber and loading the back of
his pick up truck. Pretty Jane arrives carrying a tin of
cookies. She notices Jes is not his usual cheery self.

                    PRETTY JANE
          Now you and the good professor
          enjoy these. I made his favorite
          today, oatmeal raisin, since he was
          such a gentleman the other night.

                    JES
          Thanks, you angel.

>   PRETTY JANE
>   (Looking intently at Jes)
>   I saw something in my dream last
>   night about you, Jes. I saw the
>   Lord calling for you. Now you get
>   on; the Professor is waiting for
>   you.(she turns and waves as she
>   hobbles on) You remember what I
>   said... the Lord is at hand.

INT. PROFESSOR BARROW'S STUDY -- LATER

Jes is hauling in lumber, tools and the cookie tin. When he leans over to place some lumber on the floor, his Holy Face medal slips out from his shirt and is swinging on its chain. Barrows, startled, notices the medal.

>   PROFESSOR BARROWS
>   What have you got there?
>
>   JES
>   (handing him the cookies)
>   She made your favorite today. She
>   was all full of predictions again,
>   something about the Lord coming for
>   me.
>
>   PROFESSOR BARROWS
>   (reaching for the medal)
>   No, I mean this. It's beautiful.
>
>   JES
>   Oh, that. Actually, it was a gift
>   from my birth mother. Weird, huh?
>
>   PROFESSOR BARROWS
>   Your birth mother? Well how--
>
>   JES
>   No, not directly, I mean she left
>   this for me in an envelope with a
>   note specifying that I receive it
>   on my thirtieth birthday.
>
>   PROFESSOR BARROWS
>   Really. Let me have a look at it.
>
>   JES
>   (taking off medal)
>   Yeah, you're the theology scholar,
>   what does the writing say?

PROFESSOR BARROWS
(taking out his bifocals)
Well, it's a medal of the Holy Face, meaning the face of Christ as seen on the Shroud of Turin. It's Latin. The words over his face mean "May, O Lord, the light of thy countenance shine upon us." On the back is the symbol of a radiant communion host, "Mane nobiscum, Domine" meaning "Stay with us, O, Lord."

JES
The Shroud of Turin? I wonder why she gave me this instead of a cross or something. Maybe she is from Turin and it's a hint.

PROFESSOR BARROWS
(with trepidation)
Do you think you are ready to search for her?

JES
No. It's strange not knowing who I really am and where my real parents are. But I just feel like it would be opening a can of worms to look for her. Besides, she knows how to find me since she gave me away to Joe and Bev to raise. It's not like she has come looking for me.

PROFESSOR BARROWS
(relieved)
Well, anyway, it's a beautiful gift. You know, I have several books on the Shroud. It's the most controversial and mysterious of religious relics. I'll lend you one.

JES
(starts working)
Okay. Let's get going on these shelves. (looking at all the books) What happens here, do they breed at night while you're sleeping?

INT. MT. SINAI HOSPITAL IN SAN FRANCISCO -- DAY

Jes is standing at the nurses' station attaching his volunteer pin. NURSES direct flirtatious smiles his way, though he is unaware. Suddenly a COMMOTION erupts down the hall as a GROUP OF REPORTERS are trying to interview a DOCTOR about a controversial life support case. Jes notices one clever, attractive reporter, MAGDA SHAW, 28, standing off to the side hoping to catch the doctor off guard. She is tall and lanky, with dark eyes, a mane of dark brown hair, and an olive complexion. Jes walks towards her, amused by her attempted stealth, which is undermined by her inability to hide her natural beauty from any man in her vicinity.

                    JES
           (whispering discreetly)
    He takes his coffee break at six in
    the cafeteria, every evening like
    clockwork. (passing her, looking
    back and smiling)

                    MAGDA
    Thanks...

Jes continues down the hall.

INT. CANCER TREATMENT CENTER -- CONTINUOUS

                    NURSE
    Hi, Jes. Tyrel is in for a
    treatment. Things aren't looking
    great for him. Can you cheer him
    up?

                    JES
    Love to.

TYREL, an 8 year old black boy, sits at a chemotherapy station.

                    TYREL
    Aw, man, I'm trippin cause my main
    man Jes is here!

                    JES
    How you doin, kiddo? Okay, gimme an
    update on Simone.

                    TYREL
          Man she's ten and I'm only eight.
          No way she's even gonna look at me,
          specially with this baldy ole head
          a mine.

                    JES
          Are you kidding, bald is so cool
          right now.

Tyrel notices Jes' medal.

                    TYREL
          Awesome! That's my man Jesus. Can I
          wear it for a little while? Maybe
          it can help me get better. You
          think I'm gonna get better, Jes?

                    JES
               (putting medal over
                Tyrel's head)
          Not only do I think you'll get
          better, but I think you'll be
          taking Simone to an A's game this
          season.

                    TYREL
          Whatch you talkin about? You don't
          have no girlfriend neither. Tell
          you what, you git a woman and we'll
          all go together.

                    JES
          Deal. But first I'm getting the
          cookie tray filled. You relax now.
          I'll be right back with some ginger
          snaps.

INT. GREYSON PSYCHIATRIC CENTER -- DAY

Professor Barrows is walking down the hall with GRACE, 25, an employee at the center. They enter MARIA PIERINA's room.

                    GRACE
          She's about the same as last week.

Maria, 54 and Italian, is kneeling before a picture of Christ, wearing a makeshift nun's habit of scarves and MUMBLING PRAYERS.

GRACE
Sister Pierina, your cousin is here.
    (whispers to Barrows)
She insists on being called "Sister" now.

PROFESSOR BARROWS
Thank you, Grace. I'll take it from here.

Grace departs.

PROFESSOR BARROWS
"Sister" Pierina? You are a piece of work. I have to hand it to you, the theatrics are brilliant. Really, Maria, I don't know how you have managed this for five years. How did I ever let you talk me into having you committed?

MARIA
    (strong Italian accent)
Shh. Now tell me, how was his birthday party? Did they give him the medal?

PROFESSOR BARROWS
Yes, he was wearing it the other day. But don't worry, he still has no plans to search for you.

MARIA
Oh, thank God! But such a mixed blessing this news. How I would love to see him, but I know it is not safe. Listen to me, Edward, I am so worried about him. I have had dreams the past few nights where they are coming for him.

PROFESSOR BARROWS
Maria, these are anxiety dreams. He just turned thirty; it's natural that you would have them now. I will continue to look after him. I promise.

MARIA
Yes. Alright. I am sorry. I think the medal has made me remember all of the years of running and hiding.

                    MARIA (CONT'D)
          I do not want him to go through
          that too.

Professor Barrows embraces her and nuzzles his face into her
neck and long hair, breathing in her scent.

INT. PRESS CONFERENCE ROOM IN TURIN -- NIGHT

Stella, Lorenzo, and August are offstage reviewing their
notes for the impending conference. CARDINAL CAVELLI, an
eminent, fifty year old Vatican official, enters and
approaches them. Though caught off guard, they feign
confidence.

                    CARDINAL CAVELLI
          I don't know what you three are up
          to, but I warn you, if you or
          Viviano did any unauthorized
          experiments on the Sindone, you
          will be facing serious
          consequences.

                    STELLA
          You will find out soon enough,
          Cardinal, as will the rest of the
          world.

                    ANNOUNCER (OFF SCREEN)
          Let me get our panel of experts in
          here so we can begin.

                    STELLA
          That's our cue, gentlemen.

Stella winks at Cardinal Cavelli as the three enter the
conference room, overflowing with REPORTERS.

                    ANNOUNCER
              (televising begins)
          Good evening. Tonight we have a
          special announcement from three
          esteemed colleagues of the late
          Sindonologist, radiologist and
          paleogeneticist, Vincenze Viviano.
          Allow me to introduce his wife,
          Dr. Stella Forbes, an American
          reproductive endocrinologist;
          Dr. Lorenzo Botari, Turin's own
          renown Sindonologist and nuclear
          biologist; and Dr. August Parker,
          an American Sindonologist and
          chemist.

ANNOUNCER (CONT'D)
For our audience, 'Sindonologist' is the title given to any expert who studies our most famous religious relic, the Sindone, known to most as the Shroud of Turin. Dr. Forbes, please. (steps aside for Stella)

STELLA
Thank you. Good evening. My colleagues and I are here tonight to announce the release of my late husband's research notes on his secret experiments with blood samples extracted from the Shroud of Turin. (GASPS from the AUDIENCE) Vincenze Viviano was a brilliant man with a vision far beyond that of his contemporaries. In the late 1970's, Dr. Viviano took part in a research project on the Shroud. He was given threads from the Shroud which contained human blood stains. In possession of these samples and with his long time interest in eugenic experimentation, he sought out the help of Dr. Parker and Dr. Botari. The three of them launched a secret experiment in an attempt to clone the DNA extracted from the blood cells. (incredulous REPORTERS LAUGH) As you well know, it is only possible to clone active cells, thus they used radiation treatments to animate the cells. Their experiments were miraculously successful, as Dr. Viviano's research notes will prove. (Cardinal Cavelli shoots her a threatening look) At this stage, I assisted in furthering the experiment by implanting the cloned DNA into an egg, via in vitro fertilization. The host of this egg was Maria Botari, Dr. Botari's wife. Mrs. Botari became pregnant and was in her seventh month when she disappeared.

Lorenzo and August place an enlarged photo of Maria on an easel. Reporters RUMBLE and stir in their seats.

REPORTER 1
Dr. Forbes, are you saying--

STELLA
Please, let me finish. We are unsure why Mrs. Botari disappeared, but Dr. Botari hired a private investigator in an effort to locate her. We know she went to America. We assume she had the child. Five years ago she was seen in northern California, but managed to elude us again. This photograph was taken when Maria was twenty-four. She is now fifty-four. I realize you all will have many questions and doubts about the validity of what we are saying. That is why we are appealing for help in locating Mrs. Botari and her child, who is now thirty years old. If you have any information on the whereabouts of Maria Botari, please contact the number on your screen. Thank you. We will take no questions at this time.

REPORTER 2
You are telling us a clone of Jesus Christ is out there and you won't take any questions!?

LORENZO
(approaching podium)
We are telling you that there is a clone of the man of the Shroud out there. It has never been proven that the image on the Shroud is that of Jesus Christ. But the sooner we find my wife, the sooner we will have answers. Thank you.

Stella, August, and Lorenzo walk out of the conference room as a COMMOTION ensues and reporters are hungry for more information. Cardinal Cavelli is in the back corner of the room TALKING DISCREETLY on his cell phone.

CARDINAL CAVELLI
Get the jet ready. We are leaving for San Francisco immediately.

INT. MAGDA'S SAN FRANCISCO APARTMENT -- MORNING

Magda enters her apartment, just home from her morning run. She is cooling down when her CELL PHONE RINGS.

JOSH (VOICE OVER)
Thank God I found you! Turn on your TV. You are gonna *freak*!

Magda turns on the TV and watches NEWS ABOUT PRESS CONFERENCE.

MAGDA
I just got home. Oh my God. (laughs) The Shroud of Turin, the story that keeps on giving!

JOSH
I know, can you believe this? You lucky bitch that you ran that series of articles on it last year. Oh, my God, goose bumps!

MAGDA
Calm down, drama queen.

JOSH
Hey, watch it.

MAGDA
Oh, that's right. Hang on, my land line is ringing.

Magda runs to pick up her RINGING PHONE.

MAGDA
Hello?

GRACE (VOICE OVER)
Mag, it's Grace. Have you seen the news?

MAGDA
Yeah, I've got it on now.

Maria's picture is shown on the TV.

GRACE
Look, look now! Do you see her? I'm almost positive she is one of our patients. The photo is old, but see that mole on her neck on the right. Mag, I think you should get up here quickly and check this out. I'll turn off the TV so no one else sees this. Hurry!

Magda hangs up with Grace, grabs her cell phone and completes her conversation with Josh.

          MAGDA
I'll pick you up. We're going to Santa Rosa.

INT. THE ADLER'S HOUSE IN SAN FRANCISCO -- CONTINUOUS

Bev is in the kitchen making breakfast while Joe is in his home office studying acupuncture charts and practicing on himself with needles. The TV is on in the kitchen and a local station is BROADCASTING THE STORY with Maria's picture on the full screen.

          NEWS ANCHOR
This woman, Maria Botari, is said to be the mother of this potential cloned baby. She is fifty-four now, so you have to imagine her aged about thirty years from the time this photo was taken.

Bev is half listening while she cooks. She looks up at the screen and CRIES OUT. Joe rushes into the kitchen, needles still in his forearms.

          JOE
What's the matter?

Bev points at Maria's face on the TV.

          NEWS ANCHOR
Again, any information you may have on the whereabouts of this woman would be appreciated.

          BEV
It's her, Joe. That's Maria. They are searching for Maria. Something about a cloned baby...oh my God.

I/E. HIGHWAY 101/GREYSON PSYCHIATRIC CENTER -- CONTINUOUS

Professor Barrows exits the highway and gets stuck at a red light. Impatient for it to change, he STRIKES his dashboard. Finally he pulls into the long winding driveway to the Greyson Psychiatric Center. He quickly enters.

RECEPTIONIST
Hello, Professor. I am surprised to see you here on a weekday.

PROFESSOR BARROWS
Yes, I have some unexpected company...uh, one of Maria's closest cousins is in town so I would like to get a day pass.

RECEPTIONIST
Usually you take her on Saturdays. I'll need the doctor's permission for today. I can see if he is available.

PROFESSOR BARROWS
Oh, I'm in an awful rush to meet her at the airport. It's just for a few hours. I promise to have her back by dinner.

RECEPTIONIST
Well...I don't know if I should...

PROFESSOR BARROWS
You know how busy the doctors are. I'd hate for Maria to miss this chance to see her.

RECEPTIONIST
Couldn't her cousin come here for a visit?

PROFESSOR BARROWS
Now what fun would that be? Please.

RECEPTIONIST
Oh, alright. But just this once. Here, you'll need to sign these papers.

PROFESSOR BARROWS
(scribbling his signature)
Thank you. I shan't forget your kindness.

The receptionist takes him into Maria's room. Maria is surprised but maintains a dull attitude until the receptionist leaves the room.

                    PROFESSOR BARROWS
          Quickly, grab just what you need.
          We've got to get you out of here.
          I'll explain everything in the car.

EXT. JES' BACK YARD -- LATER

Jes is lying in a hammock reading the book on the Shroud of
Turin. Joe pulls up the driveway and finds Jes in the back.

                    JOE
               (noticing the book title)
          Good morning, son. What's that
          you're reading?

                    JES
          Dad, what are you doing all the way
          out here? Oh, Professor Barrows
          lent it to me the other day. He was
          explaining that this medal is of
          the face on the Shroud of Turin.
          The guy knows everything. He could
          even translate the writing right
          there on the spot.

Joe is suspicious but decides not to fish.

                    JOE
          You been out here awhile? Sure is a
          nice day.

                    JES
          All morning. But why are you here?
          Not that I mind.

                    JOE
               (hedging)
          Well, you missed Master Wei's class
          on Saturday so I thought I'd come
          show you what we learned. He asked
          about you. Anyway, he taught us a
          new qigong exercise called
          "Connecting Heaven and Earth." Get
          up, I'll show you.

Joe demonstrates the exercise, while Jes jumps up and follows
along. They reach their arms overhead then bend down, pulling
up energy from the ground, continuing in a circular motion.

                    JES
          What did he say this one is good
          for?

JOE
He said it helps open all of the meridian channels and it's especially good for opening the heart channel. There, you got it. Keep the circle big. Yeah.

They stop practicing. Jes is stretching and YAWNING to wake up. Joe decides the time is right.

JOE
Son, I need to talk to you about something.

JES
I figured as much. Listen, Dad, if it's about me finding Maria, I really don't want to search for her. You guys are my parents.

JOE
I'm afraid you may not have a choice.

JES
What do you mean; has she contacted you?

JOE
No. Not exactly. But people are searching for her. It was on the news this morning.

JES
Searching for her? Why? Is she some kind of criminal?

JOE
Son, you better sit down for this.

JES
Dad what's going on? You look--

JOE
There was a report on the news this morning out of Turin, Italy.

JES
Turin?

JOE
Apparently a group of scientists there are launching a search for a woman named Maria Botari who looks remarkably like your birth mother. Your mother was certain when she saw the photograph that it was she. They claim that Maria carried a child to term thirty years ago and that child is...ah God...

JES
What? That child is what?

JOE
A human clone.

JES
(beat) Impossible.

JOE
I know, but this is their claim. It gets stranger. The main scientist involved in this supposed experiment, a guy named Viviano, used blood he extracted from the Shroud of Turin as the DNA for the cloning.

JES
(Laughing)
That's absurd!

Jes looks down at the book and fiddles with his medal.

JOE
At this point, the world is totally skeptical and thinks it's a hoax, of course. But this Viviano apparently documented everything and these three other scientists have their notes, all of which are being studied and investigated. Jes, you realize the controversy brewing here. I mean if people think it is even possible that there is a clone of Jesus Christ out there, they are going to find Maria.

                    JES
          This is too bizarre...especially
          since she left this medal for me. I
          don't understand this.

                    JOE
          There is something else. Maria is
          the wife of one of these
          scientists.

                    JES
          Okay, just stop! No way. I am not
          letting my life become some media
          circus. Even if they find her, they
          won't find me. (beat) She wouldn't
          tell them...oh, my God...that's why
          she has never come for me?

                    JOE
          Son, they *will* find her. And once
          they do they will find your mother
          and me. Your adoption was well
          documented. We live in the
          information age, Jes. They will
          find you.

                    JES
          You know what...I need to get out
          of here. This is too..I can't do
          this right now. I'm going to go
          camping for a few days. Listen,
          Dad, don't let mom worry, okay?
          I'll be alright.

                    JOE
          Take the time you need, son. And
          call us if you want anything. Here,
          you may as well arm yourself.
          (tossing him the Shroud book)

I/E GREYSON PSYCHIATRIC CENTER -- CONTINUOUS

Grace meets Magda and Josh at the entrance.

                    GRACE
          She's gone! I went in to see her
          after my break and her room was
          empty. Apparently she is out on a
          day pass, but it's weird.

                    MAGDA
          With whom? Why is it weird?

                    GRACE
          Her cousin, the only person who
          ever visits her, came and got her
          to take her to lunch. His name is
          Professor Barrows, but he normally
          only takes her on Saturdays.

                    MAGDA
          Something's up. Listen, I want to
          take a look in her room. Josh, wait
          here.

                    JOSH
          She never lets me have any fun.

Grace and Magda sneak down a hall to Maria's room. Grace
keeps watch in the hall while Magda snoops around, finding a
cross, a Holy Face prayer card, a bible, and a rosary. In a
drawer, Magda finds Joe's business card. She pockets it. She
and Grace make their way out to the parking lot.

EXT. PARKING LOT -- MINUTES LATER

                    MAGDA
               (handing Grace Joe's card)
          What do you know about this?

(CLOSE UP) JOE'S BUSINESS CARD READS:
Adler Clinic
Joseph Adler, M.D., Acupuncturist
239 Stockton Street   (415)956-1436

BACK TO SCENE:

                    GRACE
          Nothing.

                    MAGDA
          Well tell me what you do know about
          her and this Barrows.

                    GRACE
          Barrows is a Theology professor at
          the University of San Francisco. He
          had her committed about five years
          ago. I'm pretty sure he lives in
          Marin county. As for Maria, she's
          delusional but never really a
          problem.

GRACE (CONT'D)
She's one of our easier patients...calls herself "Sister Pierina" and acts like a nun all the--

MAGDA
Pierina?

GRACE
Yeah, that's her last name. It's not the name they gave on the news though. But she's Italian alright.

MAGDA
Ah! Clever girl. Sister Pierina was a nun who lived in the forties and was responsible for having a medal cast of the Holy Face of the Shroud of Turin. This is getting interesting.

JOSH
I think we should head over to this Professor's house.

MAGDA
No, he wouldn't take her there. Let's follow this lead.

Magda grabs Joe's card out of Grace's hand and SMACKS a big kiss on Grace's cheek.

MAGDA
You are the best, baby sister! Call me if any news comes in on Barrows or Maria.

INT. SAN FRANCISCO POLICE STATION -- LATER

OFFICER TATE, clean cut and 32, is sitting at his desk sneaking a look at the sports page. His PHONE RINGS.

MAGDA (VOICE OVER)
Tate, it's Magda Shaw.

OFFICER TATE
Magda! To what do I owe the honor? Oh, wait, you decided you are madly in love with me.

MAGDA
Get over yourself, Tate. Though I might consider it if you can help me out with something.

OFFICER TATE
What's up?

MAGDA
I need to locate the exact whereabouts of a Professor Edward Barrows, a theology Professor at USF. Can you track him down for me? I think he is on the run.

OFFICER TATE
I can try, but I can't promise anything. So do I get a date out of it if I find him?

MAGDA
Yeah, yeah. But only if you find him in time for me to get to him first.

OFFICER TATE
Consider it done.

INT. JOE'S CAR ON GOLDEN GATE BRIDGE -- CONTINUOUS

Joe calls Bev on his cell phone.

JOE
Honey, I found him and he knows. He's going camping to sort things out. I've got an idea. I'll pick you up in ten minutes.

INT. MAGDA'S CAR ON HIGHWAY 101 SOUTH -- LATER

Magda and Josh are headed back towards San Francisco. The RADIO is on and REPORTS are rampant about the 'Jesus clone'.

RADIO ANNOUNCER
A potential clone of Jesus Christ! Huge controversy on the horizon here, folks. Skeptics argue that it is impossible that a human clone could have been created in 1978.

                    RADIO ANNOUNCER (CONT'D)
          The Vatican is furious that the
          Shroud of Turin is being dragged
          into such scandalous accusations,
          while religious zealots are already
          heralding this as the 'Second
          Coming of Christ'.

Magda's CELL PHONE RINGS. She turns the RADIO OFF.

                    OFFICER TATE (VOICE OVER)
          Shaw, it's your lucky day. Barrows
          just used his credit card at the
          Petaluma Motel just a few hours
          ago.

                    MAGDA
          Tate, I might even give you a good
          night kiss on that date. Thanks.

Magda swerves sharply into the exit lane while Josh grabs
onto the door handle and spills his coffee.

                    JOSH
          You are the story slut from hell!
          Whoa, watch it, these pants cost a
          fortune!

EXT. THE PETALUMA MOTEL -- DUSK

Magda and Josh are standing next to her car formulating a
plan when Barrows exits his room with an ice bucket.

                    MAGDA
              (whispering)
          He looks scholarly.

                    JOSH
              (calling out)
          Professor Barrows, is that you?

Barrows sees them and is caught off guard. Josh parades over
to him.

                    JOSH
          You don't remember me? Josh Burke.
          I was a student of yours at USF.

                    PROFESSOR BARROWS
          No, I'm sorry.

                    MAGDA
          No you wouldn't. Magda Shaw,
          Professor.

MAGDA (CONT'D)
I'm a reporter with the San Francisco Dispatch. I believe you are with Maria Botari, or should I say Pierina? We need to speak with her.

PROFESSOR BARROWS
I don't know what you are talking about.

MAGDA
Really? Oh, well then, I guess I will have to bring the police in on this to find her. The Greyson Psychiatric Center claims you left with her this morning.

Magda starts to dial her cell phone.

PROFESSOR BARROWS
Wait. What is it you want with Maria, Ms. Shaw?

MAGDA
Her side of the story. I just want to talk to her before anyone else does.

PROFESSOR BARROWS
Or else?

MAGDA
Or else I call the police and who knows what will happen from there. She is a hunted woman, as you are obviously aware.

PROFESSOR BARROWS
Alright. But you must promise you will not notify the authorities.

MAGDA
Cross my heart.

INT. ROOM IN PETALUMA MOTEL -- CONTINUOUS

Maria is sitting on the bed watching the NEWS when Barrows enters with Magda and Josh in tow. She MUTES the TV.

PROFESSOR BARROWS
I'm sorry, but she threatened to call the police.

MAGDA
Hello, Maria. I'm Magda Shaw and this is my assistant, Josh Burke. Sorry to burst in on you like this.

PROFESSOR BARROWS
Ms. Shaw and Mr. Burke are with the San Francisco Dispatch. (beat) Shaw? You wrote that series of investigative articles trying to prove the Shroud was a fake!

MARIA
Edward, please, what is going on here?

MAGDA
Yes, I wrote some articles on the Shroud, but I assure you I will listen to your story objectively. Tell me about the child. Was the birth successful?

MARIA
I do not know what you mean. I have no child.

MAGDA
Look, Maria, the game's over. You've seen the news. If you did give birth to the child in question, you may as well tell me the story and dictate it on your own terms.

PROFESSOR BARROWS
Oh, and you are trustworthy; we should just take your word on that?

MAGDA
I haven't called the police, have I? But, hey, if you don't want to answer my questions then (going out on a limb) perhaps I'll talk to Joseph Adler.

Maria and Barrows, noticeably startled, CONFER PRIVATELY.

PROFESSOR BARROWS
Alright. But Maria insists that you not publish anything until she gives the go ahead.

MAGDA
You know I can't promise that; I have an editor to consider.

PROFESSOR BARROWS
Ms. Shaw, you *will* promise that or you will have no story.

MAGDA
Fine. Now let's start with the child.

MARIA
(reluctantly) His name is Jes Adler. He is thirty years old now. Dr. Adler and his wife delivered him. They were so kind to me and I was desperate so I left Jes with them and ran away. I had to protect him from those monsters.

MAGDA
Why did you leave Turin so far along in the pregnancy?

MARIA
My husband, Lorenzo, he is a very handsome man. I was suspicious...I thought he was having an affair so I took a look around in his things, searching for clues. What I found horrified me. His notes were very detailed. The baby I was carrying was not created by Lorenzo and me. I could not bear to bring an innocent child into their world, so I left.

MAGDA
Wait a minute, are you saying this child really is a clone? That's impossible.

MARIA
At first I could not believe what I read. But Lorenzo made some sick joke in his notes about going out for an espresso when I thought he was in the other room donating his sperm for the in vitro fertilization. It was so like him to do such a despicable thing.

MAGDA
Where is Jes now? (beat) Maria, you realize you have to tell me. It's the only way to protect him. If you give me the exclusive, I can help you. I'll hold off on breaking the story until we find him.

JOSH
(pulling Magda aside)
Are you nuts? This is professional suicide! Sam will skin you alive.

MAGDA
Sam is about to get the biggest story the paper has ever seen.

MARIA
He is close. But I have never had any contact with him. I cannot--

PROFESSOR BARROWS
I'm afraid Ms. Shaw is right. The only way to protect him now is to intercept him before the authorities or the media hounds find him. (beat) But please, Ms. Shaw, it's getting late and this is terribly upsetting for Maria. Couldn't we wait until tomorrow?

MAGDA
Alright. We can't risk you staying here though. I have an extra room at my place. We will meet Jes tomorrow morning. Don't try running away; I will release the story if you force my hand.

EXT. POINT REYES BEACH -- NIGHT

Jes and Sundance are outside of the tent in front of a small fire. Jes flips through the Shroud book by the light of the CRACKLING FIRE and uses his spoon as a mirror to compare his face to the face on the Shroud. He finishes eating dinner, adds wood to the fire, then crawls into his sleeping bag and lies down, looking up at the stars.

(beat) He sits up, suddenly aware of the presence of a MAN sitting by the fire. The man is his identical twin but is dressed in long robes and has a full beard and longer hair. His voice is different from Jes' and is immensely soothing.

                    MAN
              (pointing up to stars)
          There is nowhere to go.

                    JES
          Whaa...

                    MAN
          You see, Jes, you are safe here
          because there is nowhere to go.
          When you die you are still a part
          of all of this...this earth, this
          galaxy, this universe, all
          universes because there is nowhere
          to go.

                    JES
              (sputtering)
          Who are you? My name, how do you
          know my name? You look just like...

                    MAN
          When you die, you are still a part
          of all of creation. So what is
          there to fear?

The Man gets up and starts walking away towards the beach. Jes scrambles out of his sleeping bag and runs after him desperately, tripping and falling face first in the sand.

He rolls over and SPITS out the sand in his mouth as he awakens to Sundance licking his face. It is dawn and Jes is still in his sleeping bag. He sits up startled, relieved it was a dream. He gets up and starts to make coffee.

EXT: A REDWOODS GROVE -- LATER

After a morning jog, Jes and Sundance veer off the dirt path and walk deep into a forest.

                    JES
          Come 'ere, buddy. Lie down, good
          boy. It's meditation time, your
          favorite.

Sundance settles down while Jes takes a standing meditation posture and then slowly, rhythmically begins practicing the qigong exercise Joe showed him. His eyes are closed and the distinct sounds of BIRDS SINGING, DEW DROPS FALLING from tree branches, and WIND RUSTLING THE LEAVES in the trees accompany him.

He finishes his exercise, slowly opens his eyes and sees rays of sunlight streaming down through the towering redwoods.

In the distance the figure of the man from his dream is walking towards him, through the rays of sunlight. Jes blinks hard to reassure himself he is awake. The man stops and raises his arms to make his body into the symbol of the cross. The man's figure then transforms from a human cross into a cross of two bright beams of light. Jes covers his eyes as the sight becomes blinding. Sundance is awakened by the light and cowers between Jes' legs. The image of the cross of light slowly fades away then vanishes, leaving Jes and Sundance with the SOUNDS OF THE FOREST.

> JES
> (breaking a sweat)
> Time to go home, buddy.

EXT. JES' FRONT PORCH -- DAY

Professor Barrows, Maria, and Magda are sitting on the porch waiting for Jes to arrive.

> MAGDA
> Maria, tell me the story of Jes'
> birth.

> MARIA
> It feels like yesterday. I was
> living in a cheap apartment in
> Chinatown. I was so naive. I knew
> nothing of having babies.

DISSOLVE

I/E. ADLER CLINIC IN CHINATOWN -- DECEMBER, 1978 -- NIGHT

Maria, 24, is outside in the POURING RAIN having labor pains while BANGING ON THE DOOR of the Adler Clinic. Bev and Joe, in their forties, are in the clinic. Joe is finishing up his paperwork. Bev hears the BANGING through the HEAVY RAIN. She answers the door to a collapsed Maria. Joe rushes to help and they bring her inside.

Joe delivers the baby with Bev's help. An exhausted Maria is sleeping while Joe and Bev watch over the child. Maria wakes up and overhears their CONVERSATION.

> BEV (OFF SCREEN)
> Look at him, Joe. Isn't he amazing?

                    JOE (OFF SCREEN)
          He's one lucky guy. If you hadn't
          heard her out there, who knows what
          would have happened.

                    BEV
               (begins crying)
          Sometimes it's just so hard to face
          that I could not have a child.
          Going through this feels like some
          kind of cruel torture to my heart.

                    JOE
          I know how tough it still is on
          you. Maybe we should talk about
          adopting again, honey.

Maria reaches over and finds a piece of paper and a pen. She writes a note:

(CLOSE UP) MARIA'S NOTE READS:
Please take care of my baby. I cannot. God bless you. You will be loving parents. I know this in my heart. His name is Jes.

As she writes Jes' name, she almost adds more letters but stops herself. She reaches into the pocket of her coat that is hanging on the bedpost and retrieves a small, worn envelope. She writes something, places the paper into the envelope, and lays it on the table next to the note.

DISSOLVE

BACK TO SCENE

                    MARIA
          I left late that night as they were
          sleeping. I looked at him on my way
          out and my heart collapsed. But my
          prayers were answered. They raised
          him and have given him a wonderful
          life full of love.

                    MAGDA
          Professor, where do you fit into
          all of this?

                    PROFESSOR BARROWS
          I met Maria years later. She
          attended a lecture I gave on the
          Shroud. I'll admit I was skeptical
          when she first told me her story,
          but something in me trusted her and
          I was familiar with the
          Sindonologists involved. Anyway, I
          befriended Jes and have watched
          over him for Maria ever since.

Joe and Bev and FATHER O'GRADY pull up the driveway. Bev
immediately recognizes Maria and runs to greet her with a
hug. Joe is befuddled and suspicious of Magda and Barrows, as
he embraces Maria.

                    JOE
          Edward, you want to tell me what's
          going on here?

                    PROFESSOR BARROWS
          That's a long story, Joe. But
          suffice it to say we are all here
          to protect Jes.

                    MAGDA
          Dr. Adler, my name is Magda Shaw
          and I am a reporter for the
          Dispatch. I tracked down Maria and
          now we are waiting for Jes. Do you
          know where he is?

                    JOE
          A reporter? Oh, that's just great.
          Edward, what--

                    PROFESSOR BARROWS
          She's alright. We have a deal with
          Ms. Shaw that no story breaks until
          Maria says so.

                    FATHER O'GRADY
          Well, Ms. Shaw, I'm afraid that no
          story will break until the Vatican
          says so.

                    MAGDA
          What do you mean?

It starts to THUNDER. Joe opens the door with his key.

                    JOE
          Come on, let's wait inside.

I/E. JES' TRUCK ON THE ROAD HOME -- DUSK

Jes is driving through a HEAVY RAIN when he notices a drenched HITCHHIKER standing next to a bicycle. He stops and picks up AMY and puts her bicycle in the back. Amy climbs into the cab.

> AMY
> Thanks! I thought I was going to have to swim home! I'm Amy.

> JES
> Jes. And this is Sundance. Where you headed?

> AMY
> Just a few miles from here. We'll pass it on this road. Man, it was so sunny when I started out!

Jes turns on the RADIO to get the weather.

> RADIO ANNOUNCER
> Coming up the story that everyone is talking about, the Jesus clone!

> AMY
> Have you heard about this? I think it would be so awesome if it were true. I hope it is, cause the world could use somebody like Jesus right about now. We need a Second Coming. All we do is make wars and ruin the environment and starve people...

AMY'S VOICE and the RADIO FADE into the background as Jes begins having FLASHBACKS of her life.

He sees her as a YOUNG GIRL whose PARENTS ARGUE. He sees her entering an abortion clinic. Then an image of her BOYFRIEND striking her in the face. During these FLASHBACKS, a distracted Jes ignores the NEWS ANNOUNCED on the radio.

> RADIO ANNOUNCER
> This just in, the woman the world is searching for, Maria Botari, may be the same woman who has been reported missing from a mental institution in Santa Rosa...

                    AMY
          (TALKING LOUDLY over the
           radio)
     Oh, it's just up here. The house
     with the lawn ornaments. My
     boyfriend put them there. I think
     they make us look like rednecks.

Jes pulls over and turns the RADIO OFF. Amy gets out of the
truck to unload her bike. He rolls down the window.

                    AMY
     Thanks a lot, Jes. Bye, Sundance!

                    JES
     Amy...I think people need to
     forgive themselves and each other
     before the world will get any
     better. (beat) Don't let him hit
     you anymore.

Jes pulls away. Amy is standing out in the POURING RAIN,
speechless, staring at the back of his truck.

                    AMY
          (yelling)
     Who are you?

Jes sees her image fade away as he drives on. He turns to
Sundance.

                    JES
     I don't know what just happened
     there.

Jes pulls his medal out from his shirt. He starts to pull the
chain over his head when an oncoming car HONKS and swerves to
avoid hitting him head on. He changes his mind and leaves on
the medal.

INT. JES' LIVING ROOM -- NIGHT.

Joe and Bev, Barrows and Maria, and Father O'Grady are
sitting in the living room. Jes enters with Sundance and puts
down his camping gear. Everyone is SILENT, while Jes stares
at the only person he does not recognize, Maria. Magda enters
with a tray of coffee and cups. She and Jes make eye contact,
recognizing each other but not registering the hospital
meeting.

                    BEV
     Jes, honey, come in and sit down.

Maria stands, barely able to breathe. She stares intently at Jes and her eyes well up with tears.

                    MAGDA
              (blurting out)
        The hospital. Mt. Sinai.
        Sorry...I'm Magda. Magda Shaw.

                    JES
        What? Oh, right, I remember you.

Father O'Grady's CELL PHONE RINGS. He steps into the kitchen to take the call.

                    JOE
        Jes, this is Maria, your birth
        mother.

Jes awkwardly extends his hand. She smiles and takes his hand and holds it in hers, trembling.

                    PROFESSOR BARROWS
        Perhaps you two would like some
        time alone.

                    FATHER O'GRADY
              (returning)
        They will get plenty of that soon
        enough. I just got off the phone
        with Cardinal Cavelli. He will
        accompany the two of you to the
        Vatican on a private jet late
        tonight. It's the only place you'll
        be safe until all of this gets
        sorted out.

                    MAGDA
              (slightly panicked)
        Father O'Grady, you are forgetting
        that I have an exclusive on this
        story. Maria and I have a deal so
        either I come with them to the
        Vatican, or the story breaks now.

                    JES
              (laughing)
        You know, it's beginning to look
        like my life's purpose is to get
        you your stories, Ms. Shaw.

INT. THE VATICAN'S PRIVATE JET -- NIGHT

Cardinal Cavelli GREETS them on board.

> CARDINAL CAVELLI
> I am sorry to be leaving at such a late hour, but the arrangements took awhile. I encourage you to get some sleep, as we will run a series of tests on your blood and DNA in the coming days, Mr. Adler.

> JES
> Jes. Please, call me Jes.

> CARDINAL CAVELLI
> Ms. Shaw, I am not happy about your involvement. Your previous articles on the Shroud are indicative of your attitude and I will not allow--

> MAGDA
> Cardinal, I assure you I will approach this story with an open mind.

> CARDINAL CAVELLI
> I certainly hope so. Let us all try to get some sleep, shall we?

Jes and Maria are SILENT as they look at each other more carefully. Magda and Cavelli both fall asleep.

> JES
> I know I should, but I can't sleep.

> MARIA
> Nor can I. I would rather just look at you all night. My God you are handsome!

> JES
> (embarrassed)
> I've wondered all my life what you would look like. Bev and Joe described you. They said you were very brave. Maria, why--

> MARIA
> You need to know why I left you. They were coming after me, Jes.

MARIA (CONT'D)
They hired investigators to find me. I did not want them to find you too. And I swore to myself that if they ever found me I would tell them you were still born.

Jes looks away. He pulls the medal out from his shirt.

JES
And what about this? Why wait until I was thirty to give it to me?

MARIA
It is so complicated, Jes. I will explain everything. Partially it was because I wanted you to have some link to your true identity. In my faith, I believe you have a kinship to our Lord. It's hard for me to describe what it was like carrying you inside of me, knowing you were not made of me or my husband. And yet I was filled with such love for you, such a strong feeling that you belonged to the world.

JES
But you see that's just it, Maria. I don't belong to the world. I don't even know who I am anymore. All I know is that since I received this medal, my life has exploded into this--

MARIA
Oh, Jes, I wish I could be a real mother to you and protect you, but I cannot. The only advice I can give you is to trust your faith and allow the Lord to stream through the blood running through your veins. Be willing to surrender and you will be safe.

INT. THE VATICAN -- DAYS LATER

Cavelli, Magda and Maria are waiting for Jes to return from the lab.

                    MARIA
          Explain to me please, Cardinal,
          exactly what will the tests tell
          us?

                    CARDINAL CAVELLI
          Other than the obvious and most
          important, the blood type and DNA
          match, we have to look at Jes' body
          and facial structure. Computer
          generated images of the Shroud have
          given us a three dimensional model
          of the face, so we will see if Jes'
          facial proportions match up to it.
          His height we know is accurate. The
          man of the Shroud is believed to be
          between 5'11" and 6'2"; Jes is
          6'1". Eventually we will also need
          to examine your DNA and see if
          there is any match. As for your
          husband's...

                    MARIA
          I have been wanting to ask you
          about this. I am afraid of him,
          Cardinal, afraid of what he can do
          to Jes.

                    CARDINAL CAVELLI
          Yes, I understand your fear. The
          truth is that, if Jes proves to be
          a clone of the man of the Shroud,
          then we are going to have to be
          very careful in our dealings with
          your husband and his cohorts. They
          will try to claim Jes as their
          experiment, their property, in
          essence. I have no doubt about
          this.

The PHONE RINGS.

                    CARDINAL CAVELLI
          Yes? Yes, please show them in.

The lab director, DR. RINALDI, and Jes enter the room.

                    CARDINAL CAVELLI
          Dr. Rinaldi, what can you tell us?

                    DR. RINALDI
          He is a perfect match in every way!
          His blood type is AB.

DR. RINALDI (CONT'D)
The DNA is an exact match to the blood samples from the Shroud. It's incredible. His facial proportions are within ninety-eight percentile of the proportions we have from the three dimensional image. My estimation is that the two percent difference is a result of the rigor mortis in the neck of the man of the Shroud.

CARDINAL CAVELLI
Are you absolutely certain?

DR. RINALDI
I am as astonished as you, Cardinal. But that's not all. We decided to photograph Jes' face and when we developed the photos we found this.

Dr. Rinaldi shows them a negative of a photograph. There, on Jes' forehead, is a mark in the shape of the number three.

MAGDA
Oh my God...it's exactly like the blood stain on the forehead of the man of the Shroud.

DR. RINALDI
Yes. It's like Jes has an invisible birthmark, so to speak. It's fascinating.

Maria is listening, not at all surprised, while Jes is noticeably uncomfortable.

CARDINAL CAVELLI
Jes, Maria...it is time for you to meet His Holiness. He will decide where we go from here.

INT. MAGDA'S ROOM -- NIGHT

Magda is TYPING RAPIDLY on her laptop. She stops and fidgets, then dials her cell phone.

MAGDA
Josh, it's me.

JOSH (VOICE OVER)
Magda? Do you realize what time it is? Where the hell are you?

MAGDA
I'm at the Vatican.

JOSH
What?! Oh, my God, have you met the Pope?

MAGDA
No, Josh, listen...they ran tests on him and they say it's true; he is a clone of the man of the Shroud.

JOSH
What? Magda, you listen. Sam has been asking for you relentlessly. I've covered as best I could but you have to call him. He's pissed, a lot more than he usually is.

MAGDA
Alright. I'll call him now.

JOSH
Oh, right, piss him off more by waking him up?

MAGDA
Catch him with his guard down is more my hope. I'll talk to you later.

Magda dials up her editor, SAM RUFFIN.

MAGDA
Sam, it's Magda.

SAM (VOICE OVER)
Shaw? Where the hell are you and what are you up to without consulting me?

MAGDA
It's a long story, but I am in Rome at the Vatican with this 'Jesus clone' guy and Maria Botari.

SAM
What in hell? How come this is the first I'm hearing of this? And why haven't you sent in your story?

MAGDA
Listen, Sam, I am working on the
story, but I made an agreement
about the timing of its release.

SAM
I don't care about your agreement.
We can't risk the Vatican breaking
this story before we do.

MAGDA
But Sam, I would destroy the trust
I've built and betray these people,
I can't--

SAM
You can and you will or you don't
have a job. I expect an e-mail with
your story in an hour. (hangs up)

Magda reluctantly continues TYPING her story. A KNOCK. Magda opens the door.

CARDINAL CAVELLI
Ms. Shaw, I am here to inform you
that, at the Pope's request, Jes
and I will make a trip to Turin to
show him the Shroud. You are not
invited and I expect you will
behave yourself while we are away.

MAGDA
Wait. Why isn't Maria going?

CARDINAL CAVELLI
It is too risky. She would be
noticed in Turin. We will return in
a few days. Until then.

He closes the door. Magda, annoyed and suspicious, finishes TYPING her story and CLICKS the send button. Another KNOCK. She opens the door.

MAGDA
Cardinal I really think...oh...

JES
Hi. I just...well I thought I'd say
arrivederci. Listen, I'm sorry you
can't come. I realize as a
journalist it must be hard for you
to sit tight with all of this.

JES (CONT'D)
I want you to know how much I
appreciate it.

MAGDA
Uh, yeah, sure.

JES
Will you watch over Maria for me?

MAGDA
Yes, of course I will. Have a good
trip.

Jes leans in and gives her a soft kiss on the cheek. They
take a swim in each other's eyes.

JES
Thanks. See ya.

Magda closes the door and rushes to her computer in a futile
effort to retrieve the e-mail.

MAGDA
Damn it!

INT. MUSEO DELLA SINDONE IN TURIN -- NIGHT

Jes and Cardinal Cavelli are escorted downstairs into the
small, cavernous museum by the CURATOR. Cardinal Cavelli
dismisses the curator and proceeds to give Jes a short tour.

CARDINAL CAVELLI
Let's start here with Secondo Pia's
photographs of the Shroud. What was
so incredible was the
transformation of the image. Can
you imagine when he looked at the
negatives in his darkroom and saw
this figure? (pointing to encased
photos) You see, the figures were
already in a negative image,
already reversed.

JES
I read that these markings were
analyzed by forensic scientists who
all agree that the image is of a
man who was crucified.

CARDINAL CAVELLI
That's right. They discovered the
markings were consistent with the
metal tips on Roman scourges.

CARDINAL CAVELLI (CONT'D)
(showing torture instruments) They studied the patterns of the blood flow; the wounds are consistent with Biblical references we have regarding Christ's crucifixion. (pointing to marks) Specifically, the man of the Shroud was lanced in his side and both blood and serous fluid were found in this area on the cloth. The man also has the markings from a crown of thorns and he was nailed through the wrists and feet.

JES
But what about the carbon dating? Didn't it prove that the Shroud is a fake from the Middle Ages?

CARDINAL CAVELLI
Ah, now that is the subject of great controversy. You see, when they did the carbon 14 dating, they used a sample from a part of the Shroud which would have been exposed to many contaminants, a corner section which would have been touched by hundreds. Plus, the Shroud has survived two fires. And, more recent tests from textile experts refute the carbon dating, noting that the stitching style is found only in the first century Masada cloths, like those found in the area near the Dead Sea. This was reinforced in 2000 when two non-scientists took it upon themselves to bring forth evidence that Medieval cotton had been introduced into the carbon dating sample area of the Shroud, via a French reweaving technique, probably during a repair of the relic. (they walk over to charts) In addition, the pollen and dust samples revealed that the cloth must have been in Jerusalem at the time of Christ's crucifixion.

JES
If the image were man made, nobody has been able to prove how they did it, right?

CARDINAL CAVELLI
That is correct. Of course there have been various theories and experiments done, but no one has satisfactorily proven that any man, even living in Medieval times, would have had access to the knowledge and technologies evident in the image on the cloth, modern photography and electromagnetism, to name just a few. Plus, the blood, type AB, is an identical match to the Sudarium, a smaller cloth kept in Oviedo, Spain, which is said to have covered the face of Christ. If you overlay the two cloths, the blood stains are an exact match.

EXT. ALLEY TO TURIN CATHEDRAL OF ST. JOHN THE BAPTIST -- CONTINUOUS

Jes and Cardinal Cavelli exit the museum and walk towards the Cathedral.

JES
So how do you think the image got onto the Shroud?

CARDINAL CAVELLI
I am a man of God, not a scientist. I believe the image is a divine remedy which Christ left for us, kind of a going away present. I embrace the scientific theory that, during the resurrection, the Shroud collapsed through our Lord's body as a burst of radiation created the image, which is really very similar to a modern X-ray. Perhaps this is the reason Viviano was able to animate the blood cells using radiation.

JES
Wow! That's quite a theory. Can anyone prove it?

CARDINAL CAVELLI
Some scientists have gone so far as
to inject themselves with safe
levels of technetium radiation to
do so! Their results are
interesting.

Cavelli KNOCKS on the back door of the Cathedral Chapel. TWO
SECURITY GUARDS peer out from behind the curtain. A moment
later, FATHER ROSSINO opens the door.

FATHER ROSSINO
Cardinal, welcome. What a pleasure
to see you again.

CARDINAL CAVELLI
Father, thank you for accommodating
me on such short notice. May I
introduce Jes Adler.

FATHER ROSSINO
Pleased to make your acquaintance.
Do come in.

INT. GUARINI CHAPEL -- CONTINUOUS

Father Rossino leads them into the chapel to view the Shroud,
which is laid out flat and encased in a bullet-proof glass
reliquary.

CARDINAL CAVELLI
Take your time, Jes. This is an
important moment for you.

Jes starts to walk towards the Shroud but immediately turns
around, his face distraught. Cardinal Cavelli motions Father
Rossino out of the room.

JES
Look, I just don't think I can do
this. I mean I can't just be some
clump of cells that were taken off
of this cloth. There has to be more
to who I am than that!

CARDINAL CAVELLI
No matter how you were created,
Jes, you are just like the rest of
us, one of God's children. The
evidence is pointing towards the
truth about your birth and it is
irrefutable.

                    CARDINAL CAVELLI(CONT'D)
               You need to experience seeing the
               Shroud. The mystery of this relic
               has transformed people's lives for
               centuries. I am confident that
               seeing it will help you reclaim
               your identity. Let the Shroud
               inform you, not science.

Jes turns around and slowly walks towards the Shroud, while
Cardinal Cavelli joins Father Rossino in an adjacent room.

Jes walks around the Shroud with trepidation. When he first
looks down upon the image, he trembles. As he studies it more
closely, FLASHBACKS from the crucifixion enter his mind and
his eyes well up with tears. He stops before the face of the
man of the Shroud and gazes into it.

                         MAN (VOICE OVER)
                    (Softly)
               The light of the resurrection
               belongs to all of mankind. Make
               them remember.

I/E. SAN FRANCISCO AND POINT REYES -- MORNING

MONTAGE (MUSIC OVER: "HAVE YOURSELF A MERRY LITTLE CHRISTMAS"
JAMES TAYLOR)

-- Joe, walking to his clinic, passes shops decorated for
Christmas. At a news stand he sees Maria's picture and the
headline "JESUS CLONE IS REAL" on the San Francisco Dispatch.
Startled, he quickly buys a copy.

-- Professor Barrows is at home making coffee watching cable
TV NEWS when BREAKING NEWS interrupts the broadcast,
ANNOUNCING that Maria Botari and her cloned son are hiding
out at the Vatican.

-- Becca, Christmas shopping for the baby, passes the
electronics department and sees Jes' face plastered on
multiple TV screens.

-- Amy, the hitchhiker, TELEPHONES the San Francisco Dispatch
to REPORT her experience of meeting Jes.

-- John, wearing a Santa's hat, is working at a construction
site and hears the NEWS ON THE RADIO.

-- Pretty Jane is stringing Christmas lights around her planter boxes, when she suddenly stops, closes her eyes and smiles.

INT. THE VATICAN -- NIGHT

Maria is in bed, restless. She turns on the RADIO and hears the BREAKING NEWS IN ITALIAN. Furious, she gets up and BURSTS into Magda's room.

MARIA
Wake up! What have you done? Why would you do such a deceitful thing? You promised us!

MAGDA
Please, Maria, I can explain.

MARIA
Explain? Of what value is that now? They know he is here!

MAGDA
My editor found out I was here. I would have lost my job. I promise you, the story I sent him was just a skeleton and did not reveal everything.

MARIA
Promise, ha! What does this word mean to you? You revealed enough. They know his blood is a match.

MAGDA
Look, Maria, let's wait until Jes and the Cardinal return. Jes will have more control over the media if you let me manage things for him. I swear I will not let you down. I'm sorry...

Maria exits, SLAMMING the door behind her, but realizing begrudgingly that Magda is probably her best ally where the press is concerned.

INT. A PARLOR -- MORNING

Maria and Magda are peering out from behind the curtains at the LARGE CROWD below that has gathered in St. Peter's Square.

PEOPLE are carrying signs, both in favor of and protesting the 'Jesus Clone'. Some are SHOUTING, demanding the Vatican release him. Others are PLEADING to see him.

A SERVANT enters.

                    SERVANT
          Scusi, Signora, there is a call for
          you. Cardinal Cavelli.

                    MARIA
              (picking up phone)
          Grazie. Hello, Cardinal? I am so
          happy you called. We have trouble.
          It seems Ms. Shaw could not keep
          her word; the story is released.
          St. Peter's Square is full of
          people.

                    CARDINAL CAVELLI (VOICE OVER)
          I knew she wasn't to be trusted! Do
          not worry, Maria. We will sneak in
          later tonight. Jes will be safe. We
          will see you tonight. God bless
          you.

INT. PRIVATE CAR ON TRAIN FROM TURIN TO ROME -- CONTINUOUS

Cardinal Cavelli hangs up his cell phone, obviously distressed.

                    JES
          What's the matter?

                    CARDINAL CAVELLI
          It seems Ms. Shaw did not keep her
          promise; she leaked the story to
          her editor. It's all over the news
          and St. Peter's Square is a mob
          scene. Why did I trust her?

                    JES
          We really had no choice but to
          bring her along. Besides, she is
          just doing her job, can't fault her
          for that.

Cavelli is surprised by Jes' lack of concern.

                    CARDINAL CAVELLI
          You have been awfully quiet since
          you saw the Shroud.

CARDINAL CAVELLI (CONT'D)
Anything you want to discuss about the experience?

JES
Jesus was in his early thirties when he died, right?

CARDINAL CAVELLI
Yes, that's correct. (beat) You know, Jes, I have been longing to ask you: what is your religious practice?

JES
I'm a Catholic. My mom, Bev, is a devout Catholic so she raised me with faith.

CARDINAL CAVELLI
And what of your father?

JES
He is Jewish. He is also really into eastern philosophy because he is an acupuncturist. He studies Chinese medicine, you know, prickly needles, herbs and qigong.

CARDINAL CAVELLI
Do you practice Catholicism now?

JES
I'd say that I'm more than just a Christmas/Easter Catholic, where church is concerned, but every Sunday...no. I guess I'm more private in my faith. Joe has gotten me interested in qigong, energy and meditation exercises. For me that's another way of praying.

CARDINAL CAVELLI
It seems that in America there are many versions of what it means to be Catholic these days.

JES
(hesitantly)
You know, Cardinal, lately some strange things have been happening...things I can't explain.

                    CARDINAL CAVELLI
          (beat) I see. Jes, throughout the
          course of history saints and
          civilians both have had moments
          where they connect with our Lord on
          such a deep level that they become
          infused with the Holy Spirit. You
          must not fear this gift. But you
          are obligated to share it, if you
          can, to do anything to help this
          sorry world. Don't you agree?

Jes falls QUIET and looks out at the Alps passing by.

INT. THE VATICAN -- NIGHT

Jes and Cardinal Cavelli enter the study where Maria and
Magda are watching the NEWS. Maria jumps up and runs to hug
Jes. Magda has the same impulse but restrains herself.

                    MARIA
          Thank God you are safe!

                    JES
          I'm fine. You needn't worry.

                    MAGDA
          Jes, I want to apologize. My editor
          was breathing down my neck and I
          had to cooperate or--

                    JES
          It's okay, Magda. You were just
          doing your job. I understand that.

Maria watches closely, realizing an attraction is developing
between Jes and Magda.

                    CARDINAL CAVELLI
          Uh oh, we've got trouble.

Cavelli points to the TV where Stella, Lorenzo and August are
being interviewed by a famous American NEWS CORRESPONDENT in
Turin.

                    STELLA
          It is completely outrageous that
          the Vatican has basically abducted
          Maria Botari and Jes Adler!

NEWS CORRESPONDENT
But how can you be sure they are there as prisoners? That is a bold accusation.

STELLA
The Vatican has no authority to claim Jes as their own. He is the result of our scientific experiments. He's not some religious relic to be locked away by the church like the Shroud of Turin.

LORENZO
And Maria Botari is still my wife. I think I have the right to see her after all of this time.

Maria trembles and falls into a chair.

NEWS CORRESPONDENT
What do you plan to do? Jes Adler and Maria Botari are not property--

STELLA
Of course we understand that they are human beings with free wills. But we do believe that we should be allowed to see Jes in person and run our own tests on him. Why should the world rely on the Vatican's test results?

AUGUST
Perhaps it's best to bring in outside scientists to confirm or deny the truth about Mr. Adler's identity. The world deserves the truth and who better to deliver it than science. The church has its own agenda here.

NEWS CORRESPONDENT
Yes, but don't you also have yours?

STELLA
Precisely the point. Let's bring in independent, non biased experts who can give us all the answers we are waiting for.

Jes is paralyzed, seeing his creators for the first time, trying to absorb the reality of his situation. Magda places her hand on his.

                    CARDINAL CAVELLI
I am afraid they may have a point. The Church has been the subject of controversy and cover ups in the past. Perhaps it is best to rerun the tests using a group of independent scientists.

                    MAGDA
I agree. But I think it would be in Jes' best interest to have the tests run in the United States. He is an American citizen, after all.

                    CARDINAL CAVELLI
You make a good point, Ms. Shaw. Taking him out of Italy will mitigate the mistrust people have in the Church's involvement.

                    JES
I think I should face those three here first though, before going back to America.

                    MARIA
          (flooded with worry)
No, Jes. You don't realize how manipulative they are.

                    JES
That's exactly why I would rather take charge. I want them to know I am not afraid of them and will conduct these tests on my own terms.

                    CARDINAL CAVELLI
It's late. Let me discuss all of this with His Holiness in the morning.

Cardinal Cavelli and Maria go off to their rooms. Jes and Magda finally get time alone together.

EXT. A PRIVATE COURTARD -- CONTINUOUS

JES
This was a great idea; I needed some fresh air. Actually a lobotomy might not be a bad idea either.

MAGDA
You know, Jes, another way to take the upper hand is to do a live interview once the tests reconfirm what we already know. I can arrange it if you like.

JES
So you trust the Vatican's results? I would have thought you'd be a skeptic, given what everyone says about your articles on the Shroud.

MAGDA
I admit, this is all pretty implausible. I can believe you are a clone of the man of the Shroud. But Christ...I still doubt that the man of the Shroud was Jesus Christ.

JES
Were you raised with any particular religion?

MAGDA
Are you kidding? Magdalena? How Catholic can you get? My sisters both have religious names too. My parents sent us to Catholic schools and we went to church every Sunday. Then, when I was fifteen they divorced and my faith quickly went right down the drain. I don't know...maybe those articles on the Shroud were my way of getting back at them for filling my head with a bunch of lies.

JES
At least they tried to instill something in you and give you some guidance. Even if they couldn't live up to their ideals, that doesn't necessarily mean that those ideals are flawed.

MAGDA
Yeah, I've thought about that, but I guess some of the scars run too deep.

JES
So, let's see...I might be the clone of Jesus Christ and your name is Magdalena...

MAGDA
Hang on; she was a prostitute!

JES
(his palms gesturing as if balancing two things on a scale)
Prostitute/journalist...

Magda swats him and they both LAUGH.

MAGDA
So what was it like seeing the Shroud?

JES
Listen, I'm beat and it's late.

They linger, awkward and exhilarated in the moment, obviously sorry to be parting.

MAGDA
Good night.

INT. JES' ROOM -- CONTINUOUS

Jes enters his room and stops in front of the large mirror on the wall. He examines his face carefully. He dials the phone and gets Bev and Joe's ANSWERING MACHINE RECORDING.

JES
Hi, it's me. Listen, we will be coming back to the States soon to run some tests there. I'm sure you've seen the news by now. Don't worry about me. I saw the Shroud...it was...anyway, see ya in a few days. By the way, thanks... for raising me the way--

The ANSWERING MACHINE BEEPS and the call is disconnected.

EXT. A PRIVATE COURTYARD -- MORNING

Jes is walking through the courtyard looking at statues of the saints. He looks over a balcony and can see down into some side streets of the city. An OLD MAN is sweeping the streets in a small city square below. Jes watches him and suddenly his hearing becomes acute as each SWEEP OF THE BROOM becomes MAGNIFIED.

Jes has a symbiotic experience of the old man's loneliness and the agony he experiences while cleaning up after others, being faced daily with the scraps of happiness people leave behind.

Jes sees a red rubber ball in the pile of trash and he has a FLASHBACK of CHILDREN playing catch in the square. Next he sees cigarette butts and newspapers in the pile and has a FLASHBACK of a GROUP OF OLD FRIENDS smoking and LAUGHING as they are ARGUING about politics. Finally, Jes sees the old man sweep a tired long stem rose into the pile. This evokes the FLASHBACK of a COUPLE, sitting on a bench kissing and basking in the coziness of love.

The SWEEPING suddenly HALTS. The old man slowly turns around and looks up at Jes. They make eye contact and Jes nods to him. The street sweeper cannot move. His eyes well up with tears of relief and he smiles.

INT. THE PARLOR -- DAY

Maria, Magda, and Jes are waiting in the parlor for Cardinal Cavelli. They sneak a peek from behind the curtains out onto St. Peter's Square, which is again filled with CROWDS OF PEOPLE PROTESTING and PLEADING to see Jes. Cavelli enters.

                    CARDINAL CAVELLI
Alright, the arrangements have been made. We will leave for San Francisco in the morning. The team has been assembled. None of the scientists is Catholic; that ought to take care of the conspiracy theorists. Now, we just have a few hours before Dr. Forbes and her friends will arrive. Jes, are you certain you want to go through with this?

                    JES
Yes. I'd rather deal with them here in a controlled environment.

MARIA
I...I do not know if I can do this.
I am afraid I will become too
angry, yet I do not want to leave
you alone with them.

JES
Maria, I think it's best if you go.
It will just be upsetting and
besides, I'm not alone. You've seen
Magda in action; she'll keep them
in line.

Jes winks at Magda. Both Cavelli and Maria notice the growing connection between them.

MARIA
You are probably right. But I will
be nearby if you need me.

CARDINAL CAVELLI
Come, Maria, let's get you some
tea. I will return when they
arrive.

Maria and Cavelli exit the parlor. Hours pass. Jes is pacing and grows noticeably nervous.

MAGDA
Look, no matter what they did in
terms of participating in giving
you life, they have nothing to do
with who you really are. These
people had nothing to do with
shaping your true identity.

JES
(angry)
You're wrong. I know you mean well,
but they had everything to do with
shaping my identity. Don't you see?
I'm in this mess because of them.
My whole life is not my own anymore
and they are responsible for that.
Look out there. All those people
want a piece of me. What the hell
am I supposed to do now...make
miracles, heal the sick, raise the
dead?

Magda walks towards him to comfort him when the door opens and Cardinal Cavelli enters with Stella, Lorenzo, and August.

STELLA
Mr. Adler, I'm Ste--

JES
I know who you are. In fact, your opportunism has you known throughout the world at this point. Isn't that why we are here?

STELLA
Our 'opportunism' is why you have life; you might do well to remember that.

JES
Really? So that's how you view it: *you* gave me life? Don't you think that is a bit arrogant, Dr. Forbes? God gave me life. None of your experiments would have had any affect if God hadn't intervened.

STELLA
Well, I see your time at the Vatican is rubbing off on you.

LORENZO
Where is Maria?

JES
You stay away from her. She wants nothing to do with you and your goon squad.

LORENZO
She is my legal wife; we never did divorce. Does that mean nothing to the pious Maria?

Jes lurches towards him ready for blood. Maria BURSTS through the door.

MARIA
Stop it! Jes, no! Lorenzo, leave him alone. It is me you want; well I am here.

CARDINAL CAVELLI
Now let's all just calm down or I will be forced to ask security to escort you out!

Magda pulls Jes away from Lorenzo. Maria moves over to stand beside Jes.

> CARDINAL CAVELLI
> Very well. We brought the three of you here to inform you that Jes will be returning to America to be tested by an independent group of scientists who will either reconfirm or deny the Vatican's test results. Here is a list of the group and the details of the testing schedule. I think you will be pleased to see that not one Catholic is among them. In fact, most are agnostics or atheists.

Stella peruses the list with Lorenzo and August.

> AUGUST
> I know many of these names. The Cardinal is right; this is an excellent group. I have worked with several of them and will coordinate with their team for the results.

> STELLA
> Well, Cardinal, I must say I am pleasantly surprised.

> CARDINAL CAVELLI
> You know, Dr. Forbes, faith offers such immense confidence. You should try it some time. Now good day to you all. I am sure we will see one another again in America.

> LORENZO
> What, we have to leave so soon? The party was just getting interesting.

> MAGDA
> Don't forget that human cloning is still illegal. Not everyone agrees with what you have done; you might be facing criminal charges.

> JES
> Yes, and you know how we Americans love lawsuits. You had no right to clone me. Perhaps I'll sue for damages.

                    LORENZO
              (laughs)
          Sue us? For what? For giving you
          life? That's a new one; I do not
          think even an American jury will
          believe this one!

                    CARDINAL CAVELLI
          Don't forget, you used stolen
          Vatican property for your illegal
          experiments. If you think the
          Vatican is just going to forget
          about that, think again. Now good
          day.

Stella, August and Lorenzo turn to go. Lorenzo looks back and BLOWS A KISS to Maria.

                    LORENZO
          You are still so lovely, my darling
          wife.

Maria, visibly upset, turns away.

INT. TV STUDIO IN SAN FRANCISCO -- WEEKS LATER -- DAY

Magda and Jes are preparing to start a live interview.

                    MAGDA
          Are you clear about how this will
          go? Don't be nervous, it's just a
          camera.

                    JES
              (laughs)
          I'm fine, I'm fine. *You* don't be
          nervous!

The cameras start rolling.

                    MAGDA
          Good Morning. I'm Magda Shaw from
          the San Francisco Dispatch. Jes
          Adler is with us today in his first
          ever television interview. Late
          yesterday the results came in from
          a team of American scientists who
          have been investigating the
          authenticity of Mr. Adler's
          identity. The results are
          affirmative;

MAGDA (CONT'D)
he is indeed a human clone of the man of the Holy Shroud of Turin, known in Italy as the Sindone. No one has ever conclusively determined that the man of the Shroud was Jesus Christ, but many believe he was. Mr. Adler, welcome and thank you for agreeing to do this interview.

JES
Thank you, Ms. Shaw. I am happy to be here.

MAGDA
Tell us, what was it like for you finding out that you might be a clone of Jesus Christ?

JES
Surreal, as you can imagine. It's hard to believe, even after all of the testing. But I want to make one thing clear to people: even if the man of the Shroud is Jesus Christ, that does not mean, as I have heard in some reports, that I am the 'Second Coming' of Christ. I find that a ridiculous, blasphemous notion. Read your bible, folks. The Second Coming will be an event with no doubt or skepticism!

MAGDA
Do you believe the man of the Shroud was Jesus Christ?

JES
In my faith and from what I have seen of the Shroud...yes, I do. Believe me I wanted to be a skeptic. It freaks me out to be honest. But look, even if I am a clone of Christ, I'm not here for judgement day. People need to calm down; this is not the 'end of days'.

MAGDA
So, tell us then, what do you think your role is now? Does all of this make you reexamine the meaning of your existence?

JES
Sure. But I think I exist for the same reason any of us exists, because we are a manifestation of God and love, regardless of our religion or lack thereof. It scares me to think that people out there are going to put me on a pedestal. I'm just a guy, a regular Joe who can barely pay his electric bill every month and who always burns his toast. I can't perform miracles like Jesus did.

MAGDA
What do you intend to do with yourself now?

JES
Well, I recently returned to the States so I need to catch up on the details of my old life before beginning anything new. But, I guess since I am being given the opportunity to do something good, I will try to help people in whatever way I can. I just don't want people to have unrealistic expectations of me.

MAGDA
Thank you for your time. The world is obviously very curious about you and I am sure we will be hearing more as the weeks unfold.

JES
Thank you.

The cameras stop rolling.

MAGDA
Nice job. So you always burn the toast, eh?

TV PRODUCER
The phones are ringing off the hook with offers for you. This is great; our ratings are going through the roof!

Jes' CELL PHONE RINGS. He listens briefly and hangs up.

                    JES
          How fast can you get me to Mt.
          Sinai?

INT. MT. SINAI HOSPITAL -- DAY

Jes and Magda get off the elevator at the third floor. John sees them from down the hall.

                    JOHN
          Jes! There you are, man. Thank God
          you are here to catch me when I
          faint. Come on, she's about to pop!

Jes looks back at Magda.

                    MAGDA
          Go. Go!

Jes and John take off into Becca's room. She is far along in labor and they flank her bed and COACH HER TO BREATHE.

                    BECCA
          With all you've got going on and
          you are here?

She squeezes Jes' hand and then almost breaks it. John is videotaping. They COACH HER TO PUSH and she gives birth to a baby girl.

                    JOHN
          Oh, look at her! Oh, my God she's
          our little miracle.

John places the baby in Becca's arms.

                    BECCA
          Carolina. That's your name,
          sweetheart! Welcome to life. Oh,
          John, look, the two of us are one.
          She's our living love!

Jes retreats, startled back into the reality of his loveless conception.

                    JES
          Listen, I'm going to give you guys
          some time alone. She's beautiful.
          Becca, you did a great job. I'll
          call you guys soon.

                    BECCA
          It means so much to us that you
          were here.

                    JOHN
          Yeah, man, thanks a million. Hey,
          if you need a place to hide out
          from the madness, you know where we
          are. I still can't believe it; man,
          we gotta talk!

Jes leaves, deflated by the experience, yet in awe of the
life force. Forgetting about Magda, he heads straight to the
elevator. She sees him and catches up with him.

                    MAGDA
          Ditching me already?

                    JES
          Huh? Oh, sorry.

INT. MAGDA'S CAR -- CONTINUOUS

Magda is driving Jes home. She finally breaks the SILENCE.

                    MAGDA
          What happened in there? You seem
          upset. Isn't a birth a happy
          occasion?

                    JES
          Yes it is. I'm very happy for them;
          they are my best friends.

                    MAGDA
          Then what is bothering you?

                    JES
          I wasn't conceived by love, Magda.
          How the hell am I supposed to be
          the one to teach people about it?
          People are going to expect me to
          have something worthwhile to say,
          you know. I don't want this job. I
          never asked for this. It isn't me!

Magda pulls over and SCREECHES THE TIRES to a full stop.

                    MAGDA
          You know what, Jes? That's a load
          of crap!

                    MAGDA (CONT'D)
          Maria loved you enough to leave her
          husband, run away to a foreign
          country, give you away to two
          strangers, and have herself
          committed to protect you! As for
          Stella and the rest, they can't
          choose your identity. Only you can
          do that. So you can choose to run
          away from this or you can become
          who you want to be. Either way, the
          choice belongs to you now, only
          you.

Jes leans in and pulls her towards him forcefully and kisses her tenderly. (in the background) Unbeknownst to either of them, a PAPARAZZI who followed them SNAPS a photograph of them kissing.

I/E. SAN FRANCISCO AND POINT REYES -- DAY AND NIGHT

MONTAGE: (MUSIC OVER: "HIGHER" CREED)

--Global newspapers and TV stations run headlines with both ominous and jubilant reactions to Jes and the supposed Second Coming of Christ: "HE'S BACK!"; "CHRIST CLONE ON THE LOOSE"; "JOY TO THE WORLD".

--POLICE protect the barricade and disperse a CROWD assembled outside of Jes' house, eager to catch a glimpse of him.

--Jes and Magda are on a sailboat in San Francisco Bay with Professor Barrows and Maria. Jes shakes his head in dismay when he sees a small airplane above trailing a banner reading: (CLOSE UP) Sodom and Gomorrah Repent!

--Jes and Magda are at a restaurant having a romantic dinner, when, every few seconds, PEOPLE interrupt them to take a photo with Jes.

--Jes is at his qigong class with Joe and MASTER WEI. TWO WOMEN approach him for an autograph but he declines.

--A MAN with his BLIND CHILD approaches Jes at church. Jes hugs the child.

--Jes is walking out of the grocery store when a NUN makes the sign of the cross as she passes.

--Magda, alone in her apartment, closes the blinds and locks all the doors.

--An exhausted Jes unplugs his home telephone and closes his curtains to hide from lurking PAPARAZZI.

INT. TV STUDIOS/SETS -- DAY

> TALK RADIO HOST
> Good evening and welcome to the "No Bull" broadcast. We are back with Jes Adler, the 'Jesus Clone'. Don't you hate that name?

> JES
> I think it's demeaning to Jesus.

> TALK RADIO HOST
> Alright, so the big controversy from the whining secularists is that you are the Vatican's pawn in some great conspiracy to convert the world to Christianity. What's your take on that?

> JES
> Well, you always have people who love a conspiracy. And let's face it, even with the DNA evidence, it's easy to be skeptical about me. But convert the world to Christianity? No. I trust people to make their own choice about religion.

> TALK RADIO HOST
> Okay, but what about from a religious perspective? How should Christians and religious folks view you?

> JES
> As human, not divine.

CUT TO:

> DAYTIME TALK SHOW HOST
> Dr. Forbes, what do you think of Mr. Adler's claim that he is human?

> STELLA
> I am convinced that he must be. But the ramifications of this are enormous.

                    STELLA(CONT'D)
          If the man of the Shroud was Jesus
          Christ, then to say Jes Adler is
          human is to deny Christ's divinity,
          not to mention the immaculate
          conception. We may have proven that
          Christianity is founded on a lie.

CUT TO:

                    CABLE NEWS HOST
          Caller, are you there? What's your
          question for Jes Adler?

                    CALLER (VOICE OVER)
          Hi, Jes. My name is Susie. My
          question is um, I'm HIV positive
          and I was just wondering if you
          could give me any advice about how
          to prepare myself for what's to
          come.

                    JES
          Hi, Susie. I'm very sorry to hear
          that. Well, first let me ask you,
          do you have any religion or
          spiritual practice that you draw
          strength from?

                    CALLER
          Well, no. I'm kind of an atheist.

                    JES
          Then I would suggest finding
          whatever it is that makes you feel
          the most connected to life. Maybe
          it's your family or friends or
          being in nature. Whatever it is,
          give that to yourself as much as
          possible. I wish you the best.

CUT TO:

                    NATIONAL NEWS ANCHOR
          Cardinal, how does the Vatican
          reconcile Jes Adler's rather all
          encompassing message? While he's
          not coming across as an opponent of
          the Vatican and Catholicism, nor is
          he spreading a firm message of
          Christianity.

CARDINAL CAVELLI
Jes is a Catholic and has been his whole life. But I believe he is in a difficult position and, from what I know of him, he does not wish to alienate people. I have faith in Jes. I believe eventually he will embrace a more specific message, one that is more centered around Christianity.

NATIONAL NEWS ANCHOR
Meanwhile, I hear that the Vatican has been flooded with claims of supposed 'miracles'. Is that true?

CARDINAL CAVELLI
(sighs heavily)
Yes. Too many for us to investigate actually. Jes denies all of them, of course. But people insist on believing he is Christ come again.

NATIONAL NEWS ANCHOR
Do you believe he is Christ come again?

CARDINAL CAVELLI
Absolutely not, nor does he. But I do believe Jes may be a messenger, sent by our Lord.

CUT TO:

TV EVANGALIST
(showing photo of Jes and Magda kissing)
Look at this filth! She is defiling the good name of the offspring of the holiest and only, Jesus Christ. Why, she even bears the name of the whore!

CUT TO:

EXT. IN FRONT OF MAGDA'S APARTMENT BUILDING -- DAY

PROTESTORS are carrying signs and CHANTING.

PROTESTORS
Stay away from Jes! Stay away from Jes!

INT. THE ADLER'S HOUSE -- NIGHT

Jes and Bev are sitting by the fire in the living room. Sundance is curled up on the floor beside Jes.

BEV
You are so quiet, honey. Anything wrong?

JES
I'm just wiped out. It's amazing how out of control this is becoming.

He shows Bev the photo in the newspaper of him kissing Magda.

BEV
No doubt having a private life isn't going to be easy for awhile. But over time, this story will fade into the background like the rest of them.

JES
Yeah, but meanwhile Magda doesn't think it's a good idea for us to see each other. She can barely get in and out of her apartment.

BEV
You really care for her, don't you.

JES
I don't know. Yes. But it's all tainted by everything that's happening. Nothing in my life feels natural anymore.

BEV
Jes, I think the most important thing to remember is to be yourself through all of this.

JES
How? Every word that comes out of my mouth is monitored and scrutinized.

JES (CONT'D)
If I come off as being too Christian, I risk alienating people and the secularists go after me. If I am too all inclusive in my message, then I betray the Church and my faith. If I try to have a relationship, the woman I care about is attacked and accused of being a whore. I don't have the luxury of privacy or anonymity anymore. I don't even have the luxury of having my own beliefs or opinions!

BEV
Of course you do. You are promoting religious tolerance, that's all. Jes, you have to listen to your own heart and trust yourself, honey.

INT. JES' CHILDHOOD BEDROOM -- LATER

Jes is lying in bed reading about the Shroud. He falls asleep with the book on his chest and begins dreaming.

EXT. A MAZE -- DAY

In his dream, Jes is walking through a maze of stained glass walls. The VIRGIN MARY appears from out of the refracting light and stands before him.

VIRGIN MARY
You are the reminder of the light of His resurrection, yet the truth of your origins lies in the darkest recesses of man's nature. Reconcile the darkness with the light.

The dream switches to Maria, CRYING OUT for help as she runs through the maze in a heavy fog being chased by Lorenzo. Jes is unable to find her. Stella appears, holding a newborn.

STELLA
(to infant)
You belong to me now. No one can protect you. (laughing eerily)

The newborn begins to transform into a bundle of light in Stella's hands. She hands him to Maria. Stella and Lorenzo then run for their lives SCREAMING.

BACK TO SCENE:

Jes is fitful in his bed and the Shroud book falls to the floor. He awakens, drenched in sweat. He reaches over to the bed table for a pen and picks up the book and writes on a page:
(CLOSE UP) Reconcile the darkness with the light.

I/E. THE ADLER'S KITCHEN/FRONT PORCH -- MORNING

Bev and Joe are eating breakfast. Jes enters, distracted but in a better mood.

>   JOE
> Well there he is! You slept a long
> time, son.

>   JES
> Guess I needed it. What smells so
> good?

>   BEV
> Sit down, honey, I made pancakes.

>   JES
> Pancakes? Wow, the royal treatment.
> I think I'll have to stay here more
> often. I know Sundance loves how
> you spoil him. Isn't that right,
> buddy?

Jes pets Sundance and starts eating breakfast when there is a KNOCK ON THE FRONT DOOR. Bev starts to get up.

>   JES
> Sit, mom, I'll get it.

Jes walks to the door and sees Stella through the glass. He hesitates and opens the door.

>   JES
> What do you want, Stella?

>   STELLA
> Good morning to you too. (beat) May
> I come in?

Jes walks out onto the front porch and closes the door behind him.

STELLA
Very well. I thought we should talk.

JES
About what?

STELLA
Viviano, for starters. Aren't you the least bit curious as to why he experimented on the blood samples?

JES
Stella, what is it you're after here? Get to the point.

STELLA
My late husband was obsessed with the Shroud. He was certain that the mystery would be solved if the cloning were successful. And he was right; we know the truth now. Christ was not divine. If he were, then you would be too.

JES
Okay, let me get this straight. On the one hand, you're saying that the man of the Shroud was Jesus Christ. On the other hand, you claim Christ was not divine. What was he then, Houdini? How did the image get onto the Shroud if it's not man made and Christ was not divine?

STELLA
I cannot explain how the image got onto the Shroud. But someone could if the Vatican would authorize more experimentation.

JES
Let me ask you something, Stella. Maria told me that in Lorenzo's notes he wrote that the plan was to keep my identity a secret until I was thirty years old. Why? What exactly was your plan for me?

STELLA
We had to keep you a secret! In 1978, Somatic Cell Nuclear Transfer had not been developed. Viviano accomplished this way before its time; no one would have accepted his work. We would have been driven out of Italy and accused of heresy. Plus, there was so much controversy regarding the validity of the Shroud. We would have been laughed out of Turin for suggesting that the blood cells were miraculously animated.

JES
Okay, okay. That might have been part of your reasoning. But age thirty? I think you all wanted to claim to the world that you created the Second Coming of Christ, just in case I did turn out to be divine. (laughs) You actually had the audacity to think that you could have the Second Coming on your own terms! And you have the arrogance to stand here now and pretend that you were just trying to prove that Christ was human and Christianity is a farce!

STELLA
Alright, if you want the truth, we didn't know for sure if you would be divine or not. But we do now! Tell me, Jes, how do you live with your own hypocrisy?

JES
Unlike you, I don't need scientific proof to explain Christ's divinity. Faith is enough for me, Stella. What I do have a hard time living with is the fact that I was created out of your evil intentions and not by love. That repulses me! The only love involved was Maria, who had the guts to stand up to you lunatics.

STELLA
She was just the woman who carried you.

STELLA (CONT'D)
I created you in a dish and implanted you into her womb. That's the reality, like it or not! As they say, "You can't choose your parents."

JES
No, you can't choose your parents. But you can choose if you want to have a relationship with them. The only people I consider my parents are Joe, Bev and Maria. Now get out of my sight.

Furious, Stella starts to leave but has to have the last word.

STELLA
As for the 'Second Coming', why shouldn't science dictate the terms of religion? Religion has been dictating the terms of science for centuries. (beat) And here you are, expending so much energy trying to prove you are only human when the world is begging to believe you are divine. Why not just claim divinity? Think of the power you could have and the good you could do.

JES
Oh, so attempting to destroy Christianity is not enough power for you? You need to reign over divinity too? You can't have it both ways, Stella.

STELLA
Nor can you.

EXT. STREETS FROM NORTH BEACH TO PACIFIC HEIGHTS -- DUSK

(MUSIC OVER: "X-STATIC PROCESS" MADONNA)

Jes is walking from the Adler's house to Magda's apartment. He passes a HOMELESS MAN passed out on the sidewalk, an empty bottle beside him. He sees a COUPLE ARGUING and crosses the street to avoid them. Tired faces of PEOPLE on their way home from work pass him. A group of KIDS are huddled in a playground passing a crack pipe. A newspaper machine carries the day's headline: "NORTH KOREA THREATENS SECOND NUCLEAR TEST".

Jes looks in the window of a small neighborhood restaurant and sees Magda inside with Officer Tate. They are having dinner and look very comfortable with each other. Jes starts to enter but changes his mind.

EXT. THE MARIN HEADLANDS -- MORNING

Jes, Joe and Sundance take a walk on top of an old military fortress overlooking the ocean. Jes is QUIET and distant.

>   JOE
> You know, son, your mother has this faith that drives her spirit and comforts her at every turn. Although we have different takes on religion, we both believe that God is hidden in all things. Right now, you have to leave behind all of this controversy and rely on your faith. My God, Jes, do you realize what an opportunity you have to help the world heal? People listen to you because of who you are.

>   JES
> What can I possibly do to heal this world? People are so lost in themselves. Nothing I can say or do can remedy the mess we have created as a species. It's too broken to fix anything.

>   JOE
> Who said anything about fixing things? All I am saying is that most people, whatever their religion or even if they don't have religion, cannot see beyond the sphere of their own existence. I know that when you saw the Shroud, something changed in you. I can see it, son. Whatever happened in Turin, hold on to it, embrace it, believe in that alone and forget about Stella and the press and everyone else who is staking a claim on you.

EXT. THE ADLER'S HOUSE -- NIGHT

Jes is putting Sundance into the truck. Bev and Joe are outside to say goodbye. Jes hugs Joe and then kisses Bev.

                    JES
Thanks for putting me up for these past few days; I needed the reprieve.

                    BEV
You can always stay with us, you know that.

Bev reaches into her pocket and pulls out a small statue of the Virgin Mary.

                    BEV
I want you to take this. It's for protection.

                    JES
              (startled)
Thanks, mom. I'll take all the protection I can get.

Jes' CELL PHONE RINGS.

INT. MT. SINAI HOSPITAL -- LATER

Jes rushes to Tyrel's room. NADINE, Tyrel's mother, meets him at the door.

                    NADINE
            (softly and crying)
Oh, I am so glad you are here. His doctor thinks we are nearing the end. He's been asking for you. Thinks you can cure him. I explained you couldn't, but can you please just be with him?

                    JES
Of course. I'll do whatever I can.

Jes approaches Tyrel's bed.

                    TYREL
            (weakly)
It's my main man, Jes.

                    JES
              (stroking his forehead)
          Hey, pal. I'm so sorry I haven't
          seen you in so long.

                    TYREL
          I seen you on all them TV shows.
          You famous now. Maybe you could say
          somethin and heal me?

                    JES
          Well, I think I'd have to go to
          medical school before I could heal
          anybody.

                    NADINE
          Words is a lot cheaper than medical
          school!

                    TYREL
          Can you just try?

                    JES
          Sure, buddy. (beat) What I can tell
          you is that you don't need to be
          afraid at all because...because...
          there is nowhere to go.

                    TYREL
          What do you mean?

                    JES
          You are completely safe because you
          are a part of God and God is
          everything. (pulling the curtain
          aside) Here, look out at those
          stars out there. You are safe, just
          like the stars. There's nowhere to
          go. When the Lord takes you back,
          you will still be a part of all of
          this and all of us and we will
          always be connected to you.

Tyrel ponders it all as he plays with Jes' Holy Face medal.
He studies the face.

                    TYREL
          Jesus suffered a lot, didn't he?
          Why do you think he left that
          pitcher of his face on that cloth?

                    JES
          Probably to remind us that even
          though there is a lot of suffering
          in life, we never lose the joy. If
          we have courage and faith in God's
          love we will be safe.

                    TYREL
          They whooped Jesus, didn't they?
          But I bet he didn't cry and I'm not
          gonna cry neither!

Hours pass and Jes and Nadine remain at Tyrel's side. At the moment of his passing, Nadine CRIES OUT and hugs Tyrel closely. Jes backs away to give them privacy.

Jes' body becomes overtaken by a powerful energy that has entered the room. Above Tyrel's bed, a LUMINOUS PRESENCE hovers and brightens. It is visible only to Jes.

INT. JES' BACKYARD WORKSHOP -- MORNING

Jes digs through a bucket of pieces of yellow glass, trying to find the perfect shade for the sun on the stained glass window he is making. Several completed window panes are lined across the tabletop. Magda enters and he gives her the cold shoulder.

                    MAGDA
          Hi. Whatch ya working on?

                    JES
          Just a job I'm way late on.

                    MAGDA
          They're beautiful. (beat) So, how
          come you don't return my calls? Is
          everything okay?

                    JES
          Look, a lot has been going on and
          I'm really busy right now.

                    MAGDA
          Are you kicking me out?

                    JES
          (beat) I saw you with him, okay? So
          let's not play games.

                    MAGDA
          Saw me with whom?

JES
At the restaurant the other night.
I mean it's alright. I understand.
Our involvement is probably not a
good idea for you with your career.

Magda is momentarily puzzled and then remembers her dinner with Officer Tate.

MAGDA
Oh, no, Jes, you've got it all
wrong. That was just a friend. Not
even a friend, he's a cop who helps
me out sometimes with leads. He
bribed me for a date when I was
hunting down Professor Barrows and
Maria and needed his help, that's
all. Actually, I thought it would
be good to be seen out with him to
deflect some of the paparazzi
attention.

JES
So is that how you operate, Magda?
You just use people to get what you
need? Is that why you were
interested in me?

MAGDA
That's unfair. My feelings for you
are genuine, Jes. If you can't feel
that then maybe you--

JES
What I feel is used, by you, by
Stella, by just about everyone. Why
should I trust that your feelings
for me are real and not just part
of your scheme to get a story?

MAGDA
Fine. If that's what you think,
fine!

She throws a large envelope onto his work bench and starts to leave.

JES
What's this?

MAGDA
Your schedule for media
appearances.

MAGDA (CONT'D)
I came here to tell you that Josh will be taking over handling the PR because I made the stupid mistake of thinking that we were starting a relationship and I thought it best to not oversee your schedule anymore so that there is no conflict of interest but--

JES
I don't want Josh to handle this. (beat) Look, let's just calm down.

MAGDA
You know, it's not the easiest thing in the world being with you. Your very existence makes me reexamine everything, my beliefs, my faith, my work.

JES
This isn't easy for either of us. Relationships are hard enough as it is...

MAGDA
(softens)
Don't be mad at me about Tate.

JES
I'm not. I just need to know that I can trust you.

MAGDA
You can trust me, Jes. Really.

JES
Listen, I do need to finish these windows.

Magda retrieves the envelope.

MAGDA
Can I make you dinner soon? I make a mean carbonara, and besides, we need to discuss your schedule.

Jes kisses her.

JES
Yes. Soon.

Magda leaves. Jes stops working and sits down, emotionally exhausted. He picks up the Shroud book he borrowed from Barrows then grabs his keys.

INT. PROFESSOR BARROW'S STUDY -- DAY

Professor Barrows is grading essays. Jes opens the front door.

                  JES (OFF SCREEN)
Anybody home?

                  PROFESSOR BARROWS
In here. Jes? That you?

Jes enters the office and Professor Barrows gets up and greets him with a big hug.

                  JES
Where is Maria?

                  PROFESSOR BARROWS
She's out for a stroll.

                  JES
So, what's up with you two? I mean, I don't want to pry or anything.

                  PROFESSOR BARROWS
Jes, I have loved your moth...Maria for a long time. Why else would she have been able to talk me into that crazy scheme of hers to have her committed? As soon as the Vatican grants her annulment from her marriage to Lorenzo, I intend to propose.

                  JES
That's great news! She deserves to be happy. When I think of how her life has been...

                  PROFESSOR BARROWS
Jes, her love for you is so powerful. She would not want you to blame yourself for any of this.

                  JES
(handing him the book) Here, I finished it.

                    PROFESSOR BARROWS
          I've got a few more if--

                    JES
          No, thanks. Every author who has
          written anything on the Shroud has
          already sent it to me.

                    PROFESSOR BARROWS
          So what brings you here? Are you
          looking for Maria?

                    JES
          No, actually I was hoping to speak
          with you alone. I'm just... having
          a hard time figuring out where to
          go from here. People insist on
          believing I am the Second Coming of
          Christ. It's really unnerving...

Professor Barrows goes to his bookshelves and pulls out an
anthology of poetry by Y. B. Yeats and looks up a poem.

                    PROFESSOR BARROWS
          Maybe it would help you to read
          what Yeats had to say about the
          Second Coming. He had this theory
          that life proceeded in two thousand
          year cycles. So, according to his
          theory, Christianity is nearing the
          end of its cycle.

Jes takes the book and READS ALOUD portions of the poem "The
Second Coming".

                    JES
          "Things fall apart; the center
          cannot hold. Mere anarchy is loosed
          upon the world...Surely the Second
          Coming is at hand..."

                    PROFESSOR BARROWS
                    (excitedly)
          Yes, so you see everyone is
          desperate and expecting the Second
          Coming of Christ. But look, look at
          the end of it. That's where his
          tone becomes even more ominous when
          he reflects on what is to follow.

JES
"But now I know That twenty centuries of stony sleep Were vexed to nightmare by a rocking cradle, And what rough beast, its hour come round at last, Slouches towards Bethlehem to be born?"

PROFESSOR BARROWS
The rocking cradle is the birth of Christ. But that cycle is ending and Yeats feared that something evil is headed towards us and will reign over us for the next two thousand years.

JES
That's not a very optimistic outlook! Do you agree with his theory?

PROFESSOR BARROWS
No, but I do think the world has not readied itself for the Second Coming of Christ either. We remain a disaster as a species, both as individuals and as a whole!

JES
But look, Professor, many people do not believe in the Second Coming, or in Jesus Christ for that matter. How do you reconcile that?

Barrows stews for a moment. He goes over to his chess board and pushes away all of the pieces to the side.

PROFESSOR BARROWS
(pointing to chess board)
Say you have a room and in that room you have a group of people.(he puts one chess piece on the board to indicate each) Here's a Christian, this one is a Jew, a Muslim, a Hindu, a Buddhist and an Atheist.(arranges the pieces in a circle)

JES
Is this a joke or a Jerry Springer rerun?

PROFESSOR BARROWS
I don't think even Jerry Springer would be up to the task. Anyway, What do they all have in common?

JES
Uh...they are all human beings. They live, they breathe, they will all die. They're all in the same room.

PROFESSOR BARROWS
Exactly! This is really all we will ever have in common. You allow any one of those religions or belief systems in the door and you get subjective mayhem.(knocking over the circle)

JES
So what's your point?

PROFESSOR BARROWS
Since all religious beliefs imply a certain subjectivity, rather than being threatened by that, what if people were to simply appreciate religion from a mythological perspective? So, let us take the 'myth' of the Second Coming of Christ, for example. It's a brilliant story. It's uplifting, offers hope, salvation. I don't need to have faith in Christ to appreciate the story. I can if I choose to, but the story itself still has great benefit to me because it is about personal suffering and resurrection and a second chance for the world and for individuals.

JES
It's also about a great judgement that will befall those who don't believe. What about them?

PROFESSOR BARROWS
They have free will and can decide for themselves. But the story can benefit them regardless. All humans suffer, Jes.

PROFESSOR BARROWS (CONT'D)
All humans ultimately wish to transcend suffering, regardless of their methods. What Christ teaches us is that our suffering being is also our divine being, just as they were one in the same for him.

JES
Yeah, but that's basically the same theory these fanatic terrorists use who blow up themselves for Allah so they'll spend eternity in the company of virgins.

PROFESSOR BARROWS
Interesting argument. The distinction would be though that, for the terrorist, God is hate. All of the major world religions should strive to teach that God is love. I believe that evil will always exist as long as people remain disconnected from themselves and from their own potential for personal resurrection.

JES
That's exactly why people are hinging their expectations on me now. It's easier to look outside of oneself than inside.

PROFESSOR BARROWS
Each person has the capability to be Christ like. That's why I believe the only way to ready ourselves for the Second Coming is to--

JES
Reconcile our own suffering inside ourselves first.

PROFESSOR BARROWS
Precisely.

EXT. THE ROAD BACK TO JES' HOUSE -- DUSK

Jes is driving home, lost in thought. He pulls over and walks into a grove of redwood trees. He sits down on a fallen tree and listens to the HUMMING of life around him. Digging into the forest floor, he watches tiny insects make their way through the dirt.

He uses a stick to easily break apart pieces of the decaying tree beneath him. He takes some of the dead bark, crumbles it into powder and mixes it into the earth, looking around at new shoots and evidence of growth and regeneration.

He opens his pocket knife, wipes it clean and makes a small incision in the ball of his left palm, close to where it meets his wrist. Curious and calm, he watches the blood trickling out and dropping onto the decaying tree and a new shoot of grass near his feet.

One drop of blood falls in slow motion and hits the earth. A STRONG VIBRATION shakes the forest and in the time span of one second his drop of blood transforms into the planet earth, then into the galaxy, then into the universe, then into blackness and again into a drop of blood on the surface of the ground. Jes trembles as he steadies himself. He smiles.

INT. TV STUDIO -- MORNING

Magda is preparing Jes to go into his press conference and face a room full of REPORTERS.

          MAGDA
I don't know why you wanted to do this, but can I give you some pointers?

          JES
Sure.

Jes grabs her waist and pulls her towards him.

          MAGDA
      (giggling)
Stop it, this is serious; we don't have much time. So, let them know up front that you want to speak first then take questions. And cut the questions off when you have had enough or we'll be here all day.

          JES
Yes, ma'am. I can do that. Don't forget, you owe me that dinner.

          MAGDA
Get out there. If you survive I will feed you, now go!

Magda pushes him into the room and Jes takes the podium while she sits off to the side.

INT. PRESS ROOM -- CONTINUOUS

                    JES
              (reading prepared speech)
          Good morning and thank you for
          coming. I would like to make a
          brief statement before taking
          questions. I am here today to
          announce that I will make no more
          public appearances. (GASPS of
          surprise) I remind you that I am
          not the Second Coming of Jesus
          Christ. I consider this a
          blasphemous notion and I implore
          all of you who insist on labeling
          me this way to refrain from doing
          so. You are only hurting
          yourselves.

CUT TO:

INT. FACTORY -- CONTINUOUS

A group of FACTORY WORKERS on break watch Jes on the television in SILENCE.

                    JES
          You cannot find a savior inside me.
          I am just a man. Human, not divine.
          If I have learned anything in the
          past few months, it is that a
          person's identity is not something
          to be manipulated by others.

CUT TO:

INT. PRISON -- CONTINUOUS

PRISONERS crowd around the television hanging on every word.

                    JES
          My identity includes being a
          Catholic. I put my faith in Jesus
          Christ, a popular thing to do these
          days. But a religion's validity
          should never be based on its
          popularity. It should be based on
          its message.

JES(CONT'D)
I respect all religions that
deliver the message that God is
love. And yet, even with all of our
religions, our world is still in a
shambles. Were we so fortunate to
have a man like Christ come again
on our behalf, we would embarrass
ourselves with our lack of
readiness and our stunted spiritual
evolution.

CUT TO:

INT. GRADE SCHOOL CLASSROOM -- CONTINUOUS

FIFTH GRADERS and a TEACHER watch entranced.

JES
When I consider the symbol of the
cross, I see a journey of human
suffering that one man embraced in
order to reassure us that we can
endure whatever suffering we will
face. I believe that until we
reconcile ourselves, each and every
one of us, to our own individual
suffering and shortcomings, our
world will continue to spiral out
of control.

CUT TO:

EXT. TIMES SQUARE -- CONTINUOUS

Jes' image is enlarged on the screen and a CROWD stands out
in the cold listening.

JES
But I am not here to convert you to
Christianity because I strongly
believe that you can find God's
love wherever you choose to find
it. Yet you must seek it on your
own. Have faith in yourself and do
not rely on me. I am retreating
from public life in order to
continue my own contemplation, to
study the miracle of the Sindone,
and to reconcile myself. Now, If
you have questions.

BACK TO SCENE:

JOURNALISTS begin SHOUTING QUESTIONS.

                    JOURNALIST 1
Are you saying you are abandoning public life for good?

                    JOURNALIST 2
What is your relationship to Magda Shaw?

                    JOURNALIST 3
Has the Vatican threatened you?

                    JES
Whoa, slow down. First, I am not 'abandoning' anyone. I never belonged to the public in the first place. As for Ms. Shaw, that's our business, but I'm working on it.
(they laugh) And no, the Vatican is not threatening me. Why do you jump to a conspiracy theory? The Vatican has been wonderful to me.

                    JOURNALIST 4
What about Dr. Forbes, Dr. Botari, and Dr. Parker; how do you view them?

                    JES
I am working on forgiving them and it is my hope that they will reflect on the lives they have manipulated.

                    JOURNALIST 4
How do you feel about human cloning?

                    JES
It's wrong. End of story.

                    JOURNALIST 5
You proclaim the Shroud as a miracle. What scientific theories do you subscribe to as to how the image was placed on the Shroud? And how can you be so devoted to the Shroud, yet be dating a woman who believes it is a fake?

JES
As for the Sindone, I am most intrigued by the theory that the image is a scorch mark left as a result of some kind of radiation or bursting forth of neutrons caused by the resurrection of Christ. As for Ms. Shaw, why would I judge her for not believing? Why would she judge me *for* believing? What would either of us gain by that?

JOURNALIST 5
But doesn't Christianity put forth the idea that, unless you believe in Christ, you cannot be saved? It sounds like you are copping out as a Christian here by being so all inclusive.

JES
I'm not copping out as a Christian. But force feeding people religion just alienates and divides people. It is a personal decision to come to the Lord and that decision is most profound when it happens without coercion. I do find the story of Christ's life, death, and resurrection to be an insightful lesson for anyone. That's all I came to say. Thank you and God bless you.

Jes exits the room while they continue FIRING QUESTIONS.

JOURNALIST 6
Will the Second Coming happen soon?

JOURNALIST 7
What about all the people who need you?

JOURNALIST 2
Will you marry Magda Shaw?

MONTAGE: INT. A CHURCH -- DAY

A CATHOLIC PRIEST stands at the podium, addressing the CONGREGATION.

                    PRIEST
          Jes Adler has the ring of a
          prophet. I wish he were trying to
          convert people to Christianity
          because I think he'd be hugely
          successful.

CUT TO:

INT. THE FLOOR OF THE SENATE -- DAY

A POLITICIAN addresses the SENATE.

                    POLITICIAN
          This Jes Adler has taken the symbol
          of the cross and exalted it to a
          much more democratic symbol than
          we've ever seen before. I think the
          guy should run for office! (CHEERS
          from members of the Senate)

CUT TO:

INT. HOTEL LOBBY -- DAY

CHRISTIAN COALITION MEMBERS have assembled for a conference.
They are gathered in the lobby for a coffee break. A REPORTER
is interviewing the primary SPOKESMAN.

                    CHRISTIAN COALITION SPOKESMAN
          He is not defending our Lord Jesus
          Christ as the one and only savior.
          To suggest that people can find
          this 'personal resurrection'
          without first finding Jesus Christ
          is just plain wrong!

                    REPORTER
          But don't you agree with what he
          said about not coercing people to
          find their faith in Christ? It
          seems to me he is opening the door
          for more people to consider Christ,
          whereas fundamentalist Christians
          have closed that door by angering
          people with their self
          righteousness.

CHRISTIAN COALITION SPOKESMAN
We are not conducting a popularity contest here. We stand up for our faith and our mission to bring as many people to a life with Christ as possible. Nothing wrong with that!

CUT TO:

INT. AN ELEMENTARY SCHOOL CLASSROOM -- DAY

A TEACHER stands before her STUDENTS and asks questions about Jes' press conference.

TEACHER
Carrie, what did you think about what Mr. Adler said?

CARRIE
Um...I don't really understand why he's leaving us. I think he's really cool. Maybe, um, well he could become a teacher or something and then people won't forget Jesus is coming back to help us with wars and stuff.

CUT TO:

INT. A BAR -- DAY

August Parker sits at the bar nursing his drink, listening to COMMENTARY on the press conference. The BARTENDER switches channels to an evangelical station.

TV EVANGELIST
I am telling you people, he must be the son of Jesus Christ as he was born of his very blood! And you know what's fascinatin...look at his name, J. E. S. What's missin from it? U.S., *us*...*we* are what is missin. *We* are what the Lord is cryin out foa!

INT. MAGDA'S APARTMENT -- NIGHT

Magda is in the kitchen busy preparing dinner when she hears a SOFT KNOCKING. She quickly rushes to tidy up the living room and opens the front door. In her line of sight are two hands, one holding a bouquet of pink roses, the other a bottle of champagne.

                    MAGDA
        You better not be paparazzi in
        disguise.

Jes steps out in front of her.

                    JES
        Happy Valentine's day! I came in
        through the laundry room, not a
        paparazzi in sight.

                    MAGDA
        They are really lovely. Thank you.

She takes the flowers and puts them in a vase while Jes POPS THE CORK and pours two glasses.

                    MAGDA
            (raising her glass)
        To Valentine's day.

They drink. Jes pulls her close to him.

                    JES
        Thanks for helping me out with
        everything.

                    MAGDA
            (noticeably uneasy)
        Sit down. I've got to check on
        dinner.

Jes follows her as she goes into the kitchen and stirs the food on the stove.

                    JES
        What's up?

                    MAGDA
        Nothing, I just...can I assume that
        this means things are okay between
        us now?

Jes leans in and kisses her.

					JES
They are right now.

					MAGDA
				(still uneasy)
Let me turn off the stove.

					JES
(beat) What's going on, Magda? I can tell you're upset.

					MAGDA
I don't know...it's hard to feel like we are...to know what we are doing here.

					JES
Well, it feels to me like we are starting a relationship. Granted, it has been the strangest beginning to any relationship I've had--

					MAGDA
I don't mind the strange start or the press. It's just hard when you shut me out, you know. You create this distance sometimes that feels impenetrable. Like the press conference. It would have been nice if you had informed me about what you were going to spring on us all.

					JES
You're right. I know. It's difficult for me too when I feel myself being so distant. Yet it's equally difficult for me to promise that it won't happen again. I just hope you can be patient and let me get there on my own time. It's where I want to be, Magda, but there are going to be times when I just need the space to assimilate everything that has been happening in my life. I am trying to find my way now...

					MAGDA
But you sounded so certain in your press conference, so full of direction and purpose.

                    JES
          Yeah, and it feels that way right
          now, but things have changed so
          quickly and dramatically that it is
          hard for me to feel any sense of
          permanence.

                    MAGDA
          That's what scares me! Like the way
          you got so upset about seeing me
          with Tate. You were ready to bail
          immediately, without even hearing
          my side of the story.

                    JES
          Can't you see how hard it is for me
          to trust people now? Look, please
          just give us some time? I want to
          be closer to you, really...

                    MAGDA
          (beat) Alright. Just don't shut me
          out.

They sit on the couch and he kisses her tenderly. They begin kissing more passionately and he starts to unbutton her blouse when they are interrupted by a LOUD KNOCKING.

                    JOSH (OFF SCREEN)
               (shouting)
          Mag pie? It's Josh, let me in!

Magda rolls her eyes in frustration and walks to the door as she buttons her blouse.

                    JES
          Mag pie?

                    MAGDA
          Don't ask.

Magda opens the door and Josh whisks into the room, not noticing Jes at first.

                    JOSH
          Oh, my God it's like insane trying
          to get near you, you paparazzi
          diva! (seeing Jes) Oh...hi. Am I
          interrupting? I smell something
          delicious. Isn't she wonder woman?
          Not only is she a fabulous
          journalist, but she can whip up an
          equally fab meal.

MAGDA
Josh, cut the crap. Why are you
here? And yes, you are
interrupting!

JOSH
Duty calls, my darling. Sam wants
us out at the airport, taco pronto
to cover the arrival of the First
Lady. Personally, I'm thrilled
because I'm a huge fan. She has
such an impeccable sense of
fashion.

MAGDA
She is here for an AIDS fund
raiser, not fashion, you twit.

JOSH
I know, but can't I admire her for
fashion as well as philanthropy?
Now come on, we are going to be
late.

Magda tosses Jes a defeated look.

MAGDA
(pointing to food)
Take out?

Jes grabs his coat and walks to the door. He and Magda linger
in the hallway over a goodbye kiss while Josh peeks through
the door crack for a view. Magda returns inside the apartment
and closes the door.

JOSH
Well, well aren't we getting a
little too involved with our story?
Don't forget to retain your
objectivity. Oh, who am I kidding,
he is so *hot*!

Magda whacks him in the stomach.

MAGDA
I cannot believe how bad your
timing is!

JOSH
So, tell me everything.

MAGDA
Everything is none of your damn business. (beat) Oh, alright. I'm toast, completely burnt toast! Let's get out of here and keep your mouth shut; I don't want to read about this in tomorrow's tabloids.

She turns off the lights as they exit the apartment.

JOSH
Just think, if you two have babies, you'll probably be made a saint after you die.

MAGDA
Shh! Zip it, or I'll make you a martyr!

Magda SLAMS THE DOOR behind her.

EXT. GOLDEN GATE PARK -- DAY

August Parker sits on a bench holding his briefcase in his lap. Jes approaches and sits beside him.

AUGUST
Thank you for meeting me. I know how awkward this must be.

JES
It's not the most comfortable way for me to spend an afternoon.

AUGUST
(removing a large envelope
from the briefcase)
I wanted you to have this. It won't make much sense to you, but it tells you everything you need to know about our experiments.

JES
Why are you giving me this?

AUGUST
I suppose I figure that it's the least I can do.

AUGUST (CONT'D)
Hopefully you will never need it but, for example, if you ever have any health issues this information may become relevant. Not that we expect you will...(awkward pause)

JES
What's on your mind, Dr. Parker?

AUGUST
(beat) I wanted to apologize for...well for everything. I don't know if it will make you feel any better but for years I had nightmares that you'd turn out to be the anti-Christ or some kind of demon. Like Victor Frankenstein, I lived in fear that you would come after me or my family. Silly, I know.

JES
Actually it would make me feel better if I knew that Stella had the nightmares.

AUGUST
(laughs)
I'm not sure Stella ever sleeps. Believe it or not, Jes, losing track of you was hardest on her. Stella was unable to have children. Part of her plan was to bring a child into her life. Even though Lorenzo and Maria would have raised you, Stella would have had an equally important role in your upbringing.

JES
Hasn't she heard of adoption?

AUGUST
That would have meant admitting defeat. I suppose we scientists do our best to exert control in a universe we don't fully comprehend. I know we went overboard with you. We were all young and so eager to prove ourselves in our fields, so blinded by the greed that fame compels.

                    JES
          The irony is that you three were
          really the pawns in this game. God
          brought me here, not you. (beat)
          What will you do now?

                    AUGUST
          Return to Turin with Stella and
          Lorenzo. We must face the
          consequences of our actions.
          Hopefully the Vatican will be
          compassionate, but I am ready to
          face whatever is to come. I've
          certainly earned it. I am so very
          sorry, Jes. (gets up to go) I wish
          you the best.

                    JES
          Dr. Parker... (extending his hand)
          likewise.

August's eyes well up with tears as he shakes Jes' hand.

EXT. JES' FRONT PORCH -- MORNING

Jes carries a huge pile of letters he retrieved from his
mailbox and sits down to read them. He opens the first letter
and as he reads, he can see the WRITER and hear his VOICE.

CUT TO:

INT. A BOY'S BEDROOM -- DAY

A YOUNG BOY sits on the floor of his bedroom, surrounded by
toys, petting his dog and CRYING SOFTLY.

                    YOUNG BOY (VOICE OVER)
          Dear Mr. Jesus: I know you aren't
          really Jesus, but my dog Duke has
          cancer. I was hoping you could pray
          for him cause I don't want him to
          die.

CUT TO:

INT. AN OLD HOUSE -- DAY

A WOMAN in her seventies arrives home to an empty house, carrying in her groceries. She puts down the heavy bag and walks into the living room, taking a family photograph off the mantle.

> WOMAN (VOICE OVER)
> Dear Mr. Adler: I am a widow. I write to thank you for helping me in my suffering. I had two sons. Jeremy died in the Iraq war and I lost Stephen in a fatal car accident. I am alone now. But, thanks to you, I found comfort in the Lord again, something I had lost during all of my hardship.

CUT TO:

EXT. A FARM FIELD -- DAY

An immigrant FARM WORKER sweats and toils in the field.

> FARM WORKER (VOICE OVER)
> Hello, Mr. Jes. I work very hard on a farm every day and send money to Mexico for mi familia. I did something wrong. I robbed a store and shot somebody. Mi mama needed more money for an operacion. I don't know what to do now. I'm so guilty but mi familia needs money. I cannot tell the policia. Please, ask the Lord to forgive me.

BACK TO SCENE:

Jes puts down the letter and looks at the huge pile of unread mail. He buries his face in his hands.

INT. CONSTRUCTION SITE -- DAY

Jes is installing stained glass windows while John is doing finish work on cabinets. Becca arrives carrying Carolina and a thermos of hot coffee.

                    JES
          Ah, look at her. What a sweetheart.
          Can I hold my little God child?

                    BECCA
               (handing him Carolina)
          Of course. So listen, I stopped by
          to see if you can come for dinner
          tonight. Maybe you could bring
          Magda?

                    JES
          Thanks, but I'm having dinner at my
          parent's house.

                    BECCA
          Another time then. So how are
          things with you two?

                    JES
          Uh...Magda works a lot. I thought
          quieting down my life would give us
          more time together but it hasn't.

                    JOHN
          You're serious about her, aren't
          you? Right on, brother.

                    JES
          I'd like to be. You guys are really
          fortunate, you know. Your life is
          uncomplicated and its meaning is
          right here (nuzzles his face into
          Carolina's and kisses her). I don't
          know what to do about Magda. She
          has her own life. I'm not sure it's
          fair to drag her into my mess.

                    JOHN
          Hey, "All is fair in love and
          marriage." Right, honey? (Becca
          rolls her eyes)

INT. THE ADLER'S HOUSE -- SHROVE TUESDAY -- NIGHT

Jes is noticeably despondent while having dinner with Joe,
Bev, Maria and Professor Barrows.

                    MARIA
          Where is Magda tonight, working?

                    JES
          I don't know. I haven't spoken with
          her in a few days.

They fall SILENT and continue to eat.

                    MARIA
               (blurting out)
          Jes, I am so sorry...it is all my
          fault that your life has become so
          full of pressure.

Jes drops his fork and it RATTLES on the plate.

                    JES
          Yes, there is all of this pressure
          and I don't see that it will ever
          end or that there will be even one
          corner of the planet I could live
          on without people needing me every
          second of the day! I've told them
          to search inside of *themselves* for
          their answers, but they are just
          too damn lazy! They want some
          external force to bring them
          miracles and salvation and an end
          to their pain.

                    BEV
          Not everyone is that strong, Jes.
          You can't expect people to be so
          self contained, they aren't capable
          of it.

                    JES
          Well then that's their problem to
          solve! I cannot carry the weight of
          the world here... (beat) Look, I'm
          going to take a walk. I'm sorry
          for...

Jes gets up from the table, grabs his coat and exits through
the back door.

INT. A BUSY RESTAURANT -- CONTINUOUS

Magda is having dinner with Grace at a crowded, NOISY
restaurant. Several CUSTOMERS are wearing Mardi Gras beads.

                    GRACE
          So tell me what's been going on?
          God, it's all so incredible.

                    GRACE (CONT'D)
          I mean here you have the biggest
          story of your career and that's
          where you find the love of your
          life? It's too cool, Mag.

                    MAGDA
          If it's so cool then why does it
          feel so scary? He hasn't returned
          my messages in days, Gracie.

A WAITER delivers their wine.

                    GRACE
          Maybe he's just in a funk. I mean
          the guy has become this instant
          celebrity; it must be quite an
          adjustment.

                    MAGDA
          I know, all of that is true. But I
          feel something else... like he's
          pulling away again. Just the other
          night we were back on track and
          now... we've had this advance,
          retreat dynamic going the whole
          time with each other. It makes me
          want to run for the hills.

                    GRACE
          Give it time, Mag. It's a new
          relationship. Don't do that running
          away thing you do, not this time
          around.

                    MAGDA
          Actually, I'm more afraid that
          he'll be the one to run.

EXT. STREETS OF SAN FRANCISCO -- CONTINUOUS

Jes is walking around in the city to clear his head. He turns a corner and comes upon a large CROWD out in the streets celebrating Mardi Gras. There are several neighborhood bars that are overflowing with DRUNK PEOPLE who are LAUGHING AND PARTYING. WOMEN are lifting their shirts to flash their breasts while beads are flying through the air.

Jes, caught up in the flow of the crowd, turns to head back onto the street he came from when a large clump of beads falls at his feet. He bends over to pick up the beads and his Holy Face medal slips out from behind his shirt.

SAMANTHA, 21 and tipsy, bends down simultaneously to retrieve the beads. Jes gets to them first, before even realizing she is there. When he sees her he immediately offers the beads to her. As she stands up she starts to sway as though to fall over. Jes props her up.

                        SAMANTHA
        What a gentleman. I'm Samantha. You
        wanna see my breasts for the beads?

                        JES
        No, that's okay. You keep
        them...the beads, keep them.

                        SAMANTHA
            (grabbing onto his medal)
        That's cool. How bout I show you my
        tits for that?

Samantha's boyfriend, CHUCK, approaches and sees her LAUGHING and TAUNTING Jes for his medal.

                        SAMANTHA
        Oh, please, pretty please mister,
        can't I have it?

                        CHUCK
        What's goin on here, babe?

                        SAMANTHA
        This nice man just gave me all
        these beads, but he won't give me
        his medal and he doesn't want to
        see my breasts.

Chuck scrutinizes Jes' face.

                        CHUCK
        Well maybe that's cause he's a
        faggot! (beat) Wait a second, I
        know you; you're that Jesus clone.

                        JES
        Look, it's been nice talking to you
        guys but I'm running late--

                        CHUCK
        You know what I think, Jesus boy? I
        think you are a crock of shit!

At this point TWO FRIENDS join in. Jes turns and starts to leave. Chuck grabs onto Jes' jacket and pulls him back around.

CHUCK
Wait a second, Jesus boy, I believe you have something my girlfriend wants.

JES
Hey, I'm outta here so back off!

Chuck grabs onto the medal and pulls hard, snapping the chain off of Jes' neck. Jes dives towards him to retrieve the medal. Friend 1 grabs Jes while Friend 2 punches him in the stomach. Chuck hands the medal to Samantha, who is staring in a daze. Jes is stumbling, trying to regain his balance and struggling to catch his wind.

CHUCK
Come on, Jesus boy, let's see you strike us dead with a bolt of lightening. Defend yourself, you punk.

They all LAUGH. When Jes looks up at them he sees the same men but they are now dressed in Roman soldier garb.

FRIEND 2
Yeah, you can defend yourself, can't ya? Just send a swarm of locusts down on us, you phony ass.

Jes punches Friend 2 in the face. Chuck dives onto Jes and wrestles him to the ground. Jes gains the advantage and has Chuck by the throat.

He looks down at his hand, gripping Chuck's neck. Jes then notices that he himself is now wearing Roman soldier garb. He looks at Chuck's face, which has transformed into the face of JESUS who is wearing a crown of thorns. A BIBLICAL CROWD is CHEERING ON JES. Deeply disturbed, Jes releases his grip.

Friends 1 and 2, now back to their original appearance, attack Jes again. He covers his face to protect himself but does not fight back. A MAN in the crowd with a video camera approaches and begins taping the beating, which has become savagely brutal. Samantha is YELLING:

SAMANTHA
Stop it! Stop it! Leave him alone; you'll kill him!

A few moments later the POLICE arrive on the scene and restrain the attackers. Jes is unconscious.

EXT: GOLGOTHA -- CIRCA 29 A.D. -- DAY

JESUS CHRIST hangs lifeless on the cross. The hillside is empty, save Jes who is standing before the cross, looking up at Christ. Storm clouds are passing in the distance and the sun peeks its way through the clouds.

The blood on Christ's face drips down and lands on Jes' forehead. Jes takes his hand and wipes off the blood, which has transformed into golden liquid light. The sun behind the cross now becomes blinding and the figure of Christ is silhouetted against it. Jes stands paralyzed, holding the golden elixir in his palm.

              MAN (VOICE OVER)
        (whispering)
    Whosoever will lose his life for my
    sake shall find it.

Jes falls to his knees WEEPING and buries his head in his arms. AMBULANCE SIRENS sound throughout the air.

CUT TO:

INT. AN AMBULANCE -- NIGHT

Jes is lying in the SILENT ambulance as is careens through the city streets. He falls in and out of consciousness. When he opens his eyes he sees the PARAMEDICS working on him and their mouths moving as they intensify their efforts. By the doors of the ambulance he sees the man in the long robes from his dream.

              MAN
    Remember, there is nowhere to go.
    You are safe. Completely safe...

The paramedics give Jes a morpheme injection for the pain and Jes slips away as the MAN'S WORDS REVERBERATE in his consciousness.

INT. MT. SINAI HOSPITAL INTENSIVE CARE UNIT -- LATER

Joe and Bev rush down the hall. The DOCTOR meets them on their way to Jes' room.

              DOCTOR
    He's in pretty bad shape; you
    better prepare yourselves.

DOCTOR(CONT'D)
Fortunately, he has no internal bleeding, but his face is badly beaten and he has a severe concussion, a broken arm too. He's not out of the woods yet. We need to run some more tests to make sure there is no brain damage.

BEV
Can we please see him?

DOCTOR
Yes, briefly. Why don't you go in one at a time.

JOE
Let me go in first, sweetheart.

BEV
(crying)
Alright. Oh, God, Joe, this can't be happening to our baby.

Joe holds Bev for a moment and then enters Jes' room. Jes is lying on the bed, rigged up to tubes. Both of his eyes are badly swollen. His face is scratched and black and blue. His right arm is in a cast past the elbow. Joe sits beside the bed and takes his hand. Jes stirs and looks over at him.

JES
(barely audible)
You should see the other guy.

JOE
Shh, don't waste your energy, son. You are going to need it. Your mother is here and Maria and the Professor are on their way. Son, we all love you. I'm going to let your mother come in now. You rest up.

Jes squeezes his hand limply. Joe motions to Bev and she comes in. Jes has fallen back into a morpheme sleep. Bev sits at his bedside WEEPING SOFTLY.

INT. MAGDA'S APARTMENT -- MORNING

Magda is sleeping soundly when her PHONE RINGS. She fumbles for the receiver.

MAGDA
Hello?

                    OFFICER TATE (VOICE OVER)
               Magda, it's Tate.

                    MAGDA
               Tate, what do you want? It's three
               o'--

                    OFFICER TATE
               I know. Listen, I'm at Mt. Sinai.
               Your friend, that Adler guy, he was
               beaten up pretty badly.

                    MAGDA
               What? Is he--

                    OFFICER TATE
               My partner and I were called to the
               scene. He got caught up in the
               Mardi Gras crowd and there was a
               fight. You better get over here;
               he's not looking good.

Magda hangs up and throws on her clothes.

INT. MT. SINAI HOSPITAL -- CONTINUOUS

Joe and Bev are in a waiting room when Maria and Barrows arrive. They are preoccupied as Samantha sneaks down the hall, avoiding the NURSES. She spots Jes in his room and sneaks in. She approaches his bed, horrified, carrying his medal on its chain.

                    SAMANTHA
                      (whispering)
               Hey. Mister. I don't know if you
               can hear me...I thought you might
               like to have this back.

She places the medal in his left hand and curls his fingers around it gently.

                    SAMANTHA
               The chain is broken. Sorry, I
               didn't fix it for you. I'm so sorry
               for all of this...it's all my
               fault.

She starts to CRY SOFTLY. Jes opens his eyes faintly. She notices he is awake and is taken aback.

                    SAMANTHA
          I'm so sorry. I just wanted you to
          have your medal back; it will
          protect you. I don't mean you any
          more harm.

She starts to leave and turns back towards Jes.

                    SAMANTHA
          You're not going to give up on us
          are you?

                    JES
               (struggling to speak)
          On who?

                    SAMANTHA
          You know, *us*...the world...the rest
          of you. Please don't give up on
          us...

She sneaks out of the room. Jes, squeezes the medal and rests it on his chest.

INT. HOSPITAL WAITING ROOM -- DAY

Joe, Bev and Maria have dozed off. Magda is pacing anxiously, while Barrows sits fidgeting.

                    MAGDA
          I can't stand this waiting. I wish
          we could see him.

                    PROFESSOR BARROWS
          Now we have to listen to the
          doctor. He knows what's best for
          Jes right now.

                    MAGDA
          I know. I know. I hope Tate slams
          the book at those animals! How did
          this happen? Why was he there in
          the first place?

                    PROFESSOR BARROWS
          Joe said he left to go for a walk.
          I guess he stumbled onto the crowd
          and somehow got into an argument
          with his attackers, but that's all
          I know so far. Let's see if the
          press is onto this yet.

Barrows turns on the television, keeping the VOLUME LOW.

                TV COMMENTATOR
...was severely beaten last night during the Mardi Gras parade in San Francisco. What we know so far is that somehow Mr. Adler ended up in the middle of the crowd and got into an altercation with a group of young men. We have acquired a videotape of the incident from a tourist who happened upon it and taped the beating. I warn you, it's graphic.

The video tape begins and the audio picks up the ATTACKERS JEERING as they kick and punch Jes without mercy. ONLOOKERS try to break up the fight. The camera zooms in on Jes who is doubled over and bloodied. He looks up at the attackers.

                JES
         (pleading weakly)
Don't do this. You can be better than this.

They move in and begin PUMMELING him even harder. Samantha is SCREAMING for them to stop. A police WHISTLE BLOWS, then the tape cuts off.

                TV COMMENTATOR
And there we have it, footage from our breaking news on the brutal beating of Jes Adler, the 'Jesus clone'. I don't know if you viewers caught that audio, but it sounds as though the victim was worrying more about his attackers than himself--

Barrows turns the TV OFF, studying Magda's reaction.

                PROFESSOR BARROWS
You know, Ms. Shaw, I think Jes is surpassing all of our expectations of him.

                MAGDA
         (defensively)
What do you mean expectations?

                    PROFESSOR BARROWS
          Well, let's face it, none of us
          really knew when this all began how
          he would react to this new identity
          thrust upon him. But I would say
          that he is impressing all of us,
          even you, who once exhibited the
          greatest doubts about the Shroud.

                    MAGDA
          It's hard for me to remember the
          woman who wrote those articles at
          this point, if you want the truth.

                    PROFESSOR BARROWS
                (smiling)
          I suspected as much.

INT. JES' HOSPITAL ROOM -- A WEEK LATER -- MORNING

Magda enters the room, which is filled with flower
arrangements and boxes containing all of the get-well fan
mail. Jes tries to smile to greet her, but is still too
bruised. Magda sits beside his bed and gently brushes the
hair on his forehead.

                    MAGDA
          The doc says you are much better.
          Personally, I think you've never
          looked better. I mean the color
          scheme you've got going here, the
          reds and blues, it's pretty chic.
                (her eyes spill over with tears)

                    JES
          I'm sorry.

                    MAGDA
          Sorry, for what? This was not *your*
          fault!

                    JES
          No, I'm sorry I ran out on us
          again.

Magda breaks down SOBBING and holds onto him closely.

                    MAGDA
          You know I love you. (trying to
          hold back her tears). I love you,
          Jes. I need you in my life.

JES
I love you too. Kiss me.

MAGDA
Are you sure? It looks like it will hurt.

JES
This kind of pain I can take.

They kiss softly and wallow in the happiness of the moment.

DISSOLVE

Hours have passed. Magda is sitting on the chair with her body half draped onto Jes' bed. She is asleep while Jes strokes her hair. Professor Barrows enters quietly, but Magda stirs and awakens.

JES
Baby, go home and get some rest now. You are obviously exhausted.

MAGDA
Are you sure? I do need a shower. Okay, I'll be back tonight though.

Magda kisses him good bye and leaves.

PROFESSOR BARROWS
Are you up for another visit?

JES
Sure. I'm feeling a bit stronger.

PROFESSOR BARROWS
The doctor said you are out of the woods, no brain damage that is. My, God, what a relief for you, for us all. Have you spoken to the police?

JES
Yes, but I'm not pressing charges.

PROFESSOR BARROWS
What? Why in the world not?

                    JES
          Because they won't get it that way.
          If I don't press charges, they'll
          come up against their own darkness
          and that is a much more powerful
          teacher than jail time.

                    PROFESSOR BARROWS
          You amaze me, Jes.

                    JES
          You know what amazes me? It amazes
          me to realize that the hardest part
          of a human life is to go on in the
          face of the futility of it all.

                    PROFESSOR BARROWS
          I don't follow you.

                    JES
          Humanity. It's like we'll never get
          it and all we will ever be capable
          of is this (he points to his
          battered face). Our evolution is a
          joke. Despite the fact that we have
          wonderful religions to guide us, an
          incredibly beautiful planet to call
          our home, families to love and
          protect, we continue on our same
          self destructive course. I am at a
          loss here, Professor, a total loss.
          And yet, somehow I am coming to
          accept it as our pathetic truth.

Professor Barrows mulls it over.

                    PROFESSOR BARROWS
          I am trying to remember how Joseph
          Campbell put it...ah, yes: "How
          teach again what has been taught
          correctly and incorrectly learned a
          thousand *thousand* times, throughout
          the millenniums of mankind's
          prudent folly?"

                    JES
               (laughing appreciatively)
          Yeah, but did he figure out how?

                    PROFESSOR BARROWS
          No, he left that to the hero.

                    JES
          (beat) People have to want to learn
          and grow. I know that much.

Barrows places Jes' medal in his hands and gazes at it.

                    PROFESSOR BARROWS
          Yes, and people learn and grow when
          they are reminded to do so. I
          realized the other day what you and
          the Shroud have in common besides
          blood. You both predate the
          knowledge and technologies
          responsible for your very
          existence.

                    JES
          Why is that significant?

                    PROFESSOR BARROWS
          Because you, my dear Jes, like the
          image on the Sindone, are a living
          miracle. Did you know that the word
          clone comes from the Greek word
          'klon' meaning twig or slip? I
          believe more than ever that you are
          a propagation of Jesus Christ.

                    JES
          "Split a piece of wood; I am
          there."

                    PROFESSOR BARROWS
          Yes, exactly, the Gnostic gospels
          of St. Thomas. Very good, Jes!

                    JES
          Actually I saw it in a movie. I
          don't know...somehow seeing myself
          as a twig in the midst of our
          chaotic species is not terribly
          reassuring.

                    PROFESSOR BARROWS
          Jesus Christ was *as* alive during
          his passion as he is in his
          resurrection. As his propagation,
          you get to remind our cruel, futile
          world of that simple, yet utterly
          profound lesson. And it's enough
          just to be a reminder, Jes. It has
          to be. Now get some sleep.

EXT. POINT REYES BEACH -- APRIL, 2009 -- MORNING

Jes and Magda are strolling on the beach, playing with Sundance. Jes has allowed his hair to grow and he has a full beard, thereby resembling with an astonishing likeness the image of the face on the Shroud.

He picks up pieces of driftwood and throws them to Sundance. When Magda looks away, he bends over to pick up a piece of driftwood but secretly pulls out a tube-shaped piece of brown suede that he has fastened into a bundle with ties. He throws it to Sundance and feigns that his shoulder is hurting.

          MAGDA
  Does it still bother you?

          JES
  Just a little. Can you throw to him
  for awhile?

Jes rubs his shoulder. Magda CALLS OUT to Sundance. He returns with the bundle of suede in his mouth.

          MAGDA
  Look at this thing he found.

          JES
  What is it?

Magda unties the bundle and unrolls it to find a small, stained glass box. She opens the box slowly and sees the engagement ring. Jes falls to his knees.

          JES
  Magdalena, will you marry me?

Magda can barely catch her breath. She puts on the ring and dives into his arms. They roll in the sand while Sundance jumps around frantically. Magda puts her mouth next to Jes' ear.

          MAGDA
    (whispering definitively)
  Yes! Right away. I almost lost you
  and I love you too much to wait.

INT. JES' WORKSHOP -- ONE MONTH LATER -- DAY

Jes and John are in a business meeting. Piles of papers are scattered on every available surface. Jes picks up an over-stuffed manila folder and hands it to John.

JOHN
What's this?

JES
All the orders for windows that came in while I was recovering.

JOHN
Holy shi-- hey can I still swear in front of you, man? (they laugh)

JES
Listen, John, I know your construction business has taken a hit in this economy. And there's no way I can do all this work by myself. So, I was wondering if you want to form a partnership? I'll make the windows and you install them. You can still do your other work too.

JOHN
Are you kidding, with a wife and baby to support? Hell yes! (grabs two beers out of the mini refrigerator). Let's drink to it. (beat) So how are you doin, man? I mean, how are you going to deal with all the craziness?

JES
(sighs heavily) You can't believe all the offers I'm getting. Thankfully Magda fields all the media stuff for me so I don't have to deal with it. But I'm getting approached by countless charities and organizations that want my face behind their cause.

JOHN
It's like no one wants to let go of the idea that you are Christ come again.

JES
(beat) I was thinking how weird it would be for Christ to be living in our global, internet, media infested world...Truth is, I think his message would be the same.

JES (CONT'D)
He'd still just try to teach us to be good people, to be kind.

JOHN
So you think you're gonna take on some big charity projects? I mean, let's face it, you could probably be the springboard to a lot of cool things happening in this sorry ass world of ours.

JES
I've been running so many ideas through my mind. But what I keep coming back to is the notion that all this external stuff we do in the name of charity and good deeds is just a temporary fix. Not that we should shut down our charities -- it's necessary work -- but what we *really* need to address is the interior claustrophobia we keep trying to escape from. Things really haven't changed since my last press conference. I still say we all just need to concentrate on reconciling our own suffering within before the external suffering can truly be solved.

JOHN
But how do we do that?

JES
By slowing down. By confronting our pain. By being still with it. Our pain has power over us when we try to avoid it. When we are alive in it, we transmute it.

JOHN
Listen to you, dude; you're like a disciple. (curious) How do you know this stuff anyway? Did something... happen when you were attacked?

JES
(uncomfortable) Can we change the subject?

                    JOHN
          (beat) So how's married life? I'm
          glad you finally tied the knot,
          though Becca's still pissed you
          eloped and didn't invite us. You
          guys gonna have kids?

                    JES
          (grinning) Already started working
          on it.

                    JOHN
          Cool. (beat) You'll think of a way
          to get your message out. I'm proud
          of you, man -- for holding on to
          your truth and not selling out. But
          damn you could be making some
          serious bucks!

Jes picks up one of the order forms and starts reading it. He hands it to John.

                    JES
          (laughing at the irony) Check it
          out -- looks like my message has
          always been there, right in plain
          sight on my company logo.

(CLOSE UP) Logo on order form:

Adler Glass

Let in Your Light

INT. JES' KITCHEN -- OCTOBER, 2009 -- MORNING

Jes, Pretty Jane, Maria, and Professor Barrows are in the kitchen. Maria is cooking. Magda, five months pregnant, enters. They all sit at the table and Maria serves them breakfast.

                    MAGDA
          You are so sweet to cook for us. My
          poor husband has been so overworked
          and I'm completely useless.

                    PRETTY JANE
          Nonsense, you darling girl. He'd be
          a nomad in the desert of life
          without you.

                    JES
          Don't worry about it, baby. Soon
          enough you will be busy all the
          time. Enjoy this rest.

Jes gets up to pour a cup of tea for Magda. His CELL PHONE
RINGS.

                    JES
          Hello?

                    CARDINAL CAVELLI (VOICE OVER)
          Jes? Is that you?

                    JES
          Cardinal? Great to hear your voice!

Magda and Maria gesture a wave hello.

                    CARDINAL CAVELLI
          Jes, I have some wonderful news to
          tell you. The Pope has decided to
          exhibit the Holy Shroud again in
          April and May of 2010. And he will
          visit Turin in May.

                    JES
          Really? That's fantastic! We will
          be there; you can count on that.

Jes holds the phone aside and WHISPERS the news to the
others.

                    CARDINAL CAVELLI
          Jes, you have yourself to thank for
          this renewed interest in the
          Sindone. How is Magda feeling?

                    JES
          Fantastic. She and Maria are waving
          to you right now.

                    CARDINAL CAVELLI
          Send them my love. I will be in
          touch when the details for the
          exhibition are finalized. I hope we
          can count on you to participate in
          the opening ceremonies?

                    JES
          Of course. And we'll bring the
          baby.(grins and winks at Magda)
          Take care of yourself, Cardinal.

                    CARDINAL CAVELLI
          God bless you, Jes. Good bye now.

Jes hangs up the phone and notices Magda giving him a serious
look.

                    JES
          What?

                    MAGDA
          You know...

                    JES
          (grimacing) Do I have to?

                    MAGDA
          (kissing his forehead) You'll be
          fine. I'll set it up for tomorrow.

INT. TV STATION -- DAY

Jes is giving an informal interview to a small group of NEWS
REPORTERS.

                    JES
          (looking into the camera) Good
          afternoon. By now you may have
          heard the news that the Shroud of
          Turin will again be exhibited to
          the public in the spring of 2010. I
          am here to encourage people to
          travel to Turin and experience the
          Shroud for themselves. The Shroud
          reminds us of the great potential
          we all carry within ourselves to be
          Christ-like. I believe Christ,
          through His Passion, was trying to
          show us how powerful we can be, how
          much we can endure, how much we are
          capable of giving and loving.

                    REPORTER #1
          Mr. Adler, the Shroud has so
          profoundly changed your life. And
          yet, still, the world does not know
          if it is real or fake.

REPORTER #1 (CONT'D)

Don't you think more tests should be run on it, so we can know once and for all? Turin would be a long way to travel to see a fake relic.

JES

It's up to the Vatican to decide if more tests should be run on it. (beat) This may shock you, but I've come to realize that, although I believe the Shroud is indeed the burial cloth of Jesus Christ, it doesn't really matter if the Shroud is real or just a Medieval hoax. What matters is its message... its remedy for our world. Each marking on the Shroud represents an imprint of Christ's gift to us -- the gift of His suffering. Christ had unshakable faith, so he *lived* His suffering. We run from ours. Bad marriage, get a divorce. Trouble at work, find a new job. Feeling depressed, pop a pill.

REPORTER #2

How can you call suffering a gift? Especially when it is at the hands of others. You yourself were savagely beaten. I find it hard to believe you can perceive any suffering as a gift.

JES

Exactly, we don't perceive it that way. We believe it's some kind of punishment or bad luck or someone else's fault. Christ's suffering was very real and he did suffer at the hands of others. (beat) Suffering rattles our faith. It's our highest risk of departure from whatever religion or spiritual practice we follow. Why? Because we strut around thinking we have all the control -- but we don't. But what if we were to surrender to *not* knowing...to *not* proving, but to believing? The Sindone reminds us that Christ voluntarily accepted His suffering, relinquished all control, and turned over His free will to live God's will for His life.

                    REPORTER #3
          So what are you saying -- we should
          just take suffering lying down and
          not fight it?

                    JES
          I'm just saying the only things we
          really have control over are our
          faith and free will. These are what
          give us the choice to square off
          the suffering with the joy.
          Retaining our joy amidst our
          suffering is an equal and opposite
          choice to suffering amidst our joy.
          And that choice is ours. We can
          still be kind, to ourselves and to
          one another, no matter how
          difficult life becomes. (they are
          quiet and appear to be puzzled)
          (beat) Look, I don't have all the
          answers. I'm just a man who is
          living and learning and struggling
          on a daily basis like everybody
          else. All I know for sure is this:
          When I saw the Shroud of Turin,
          something in me shifted. It's very
          personal and hard to describe. But
          maybe...just maybe the only thing
          that matters is the mystery. Just
          because we have not yet solved the
          mysteries of the Shroud and of
          suffering does not mean the
          solutions do not exist. Perhaps we
          just do not perceive the solutions
          clearly yet. Perhaps all we have to
          do is change our habitual
          relationship to suffering and...
          let in our light.

Jes THANKS THEM and walks off set while the MURMURING group
of reporters awkwardly exchange confused looks.

INT. THE HOLY FACE ALLIANCE -- RURAL UPPER PENINSULA,
MICHIGAN -- DAY

SISTER CLARE hangs up the phone and springs up from her chair
excitedly. She walks down the hall and waits outside a closed
door listening intently. She enters the small room and sees
Stella, Lorenzo, and August sleeping in their chairs. Sister
Clare CLEARS HER THROAT. The three wake up reluctantly.

SISTER CLARE
I don't hear the sound of busy
working hands in here!

STELLA
Oh, Sister, really, we have been
going at this tedious task ad
nauseam all day. Isn't there
something more interesting we could
be helping you with?

On the table in front of them is a pile of brass colored
miniature Holy Face medals, stacks of Holy Face Prayer cards,
and rolls of scotch tape. The three of them each have a box
beside them partially filled with prayer cards that have a
medal taped onto the back of them.

SISTER CLARE
More interesting...let's see, the
bathroom needs cleaning and the
storeroom is frightfully dusty--

STELLA
Alright alright, we will continue
wasting our God given talents and
tape these silly medals onto these
silly prayer cards. But I am
warning you--

SISTER CLARE
Warning me of what? That you are
ready to face criminal charges? I
could call Cardinal Cavelli back
now--

STELLA
No! No, it's fine. We are happy
little workers right here in...the
middle of nowhere.

LORENZO
What do you mean call Cardinal
Cavelli *back*? Did you just speak
with him? Did he give you any
indication when we might be
libera...I mean, when our work here
might be satisfactorily completed?

SISTER CLARE
Yes, as a matter of fact I did just speak with the Cardinal and he placed a very large order for medals that all need to be packaged individually. Two hundred and fifty thousand, to be exact. And you are just the three for the job! Isn't it joyous? The Shroud will be reopened to exhibition in the spring!

Their faces drop. Sister Clare breezes out of the room SINGING "HOLY GOD WE PRAISE THY NAME".

STELLA
(sarcastically)
"Isn't it joyous?" She is so annoyingly happy all of the time. And here I was thinking I should be grateful to Jes that I'm not wearing striped pajamas.

AUGUST
You should be. He's the one who talked Cavelli out of bringing criminal charges against us. Tape?

Stella grabs the roll of tape from him, takes a medal and tapes it onto his forehead.

LORENZO
Beats a prison tatoo!

They LAUGH and continue working.

ZOOM IN

The Holy face medals on the table are catching fragments of light. The VOICES AND LAUGHTER of Stella, Lorenzo, and August FADE INTO SILENCE.

The pile of medals transforms into a ball of spinning gold stars. The ball of stars expands outward and becomes a night sky filled with sparkling silver stars. This view expands outwards to a view of planet earth, the sun, the moon, and the other planets in our galaxy.

FADE TO BLACK.

Out of the SILENCE comes the DEEP WHISPERING:

                    MAN (VOICE OVER)
          There is nowhere to go.

TITLE: **THE END**

ADDITIONAL SCENE

INT. JES' WORKSHOP -- MARCH, 2009 -- NIGHT

It is late into the night. Soft lamp light illuminates a corner desk where Jes sits in an old brown leather chair, his hands TYPING on a keyboard. Stained glass panels lean against the wall next to his desk. They catch fragments of lamp light, causing colors to reflect and dance across his large computer monitor, which displays a written document.

                    MAGDA
          (sneaking up behind Jes, carrying a
          baby monitor in one hand and
          lovingly wrapping her free arm
          around him) Watcha working on,
          baby?

                    JES
          (rubbing his weary eyes and leaning
          back in his chair) I'm starting a
          blog. There's just no way I can
          keep up with all the mail I get --
          so, I thought I'd blog and be able
          to...maybe help people, comfort
          them, get them thinking...I don't
          know exactly yet.

                    MAGDA
          It's a great idea. Plus you've
          talked about wanting to write for
          awhile now.

                    JES
          True. (GURGLING from the baby
          monitor) Listen to our little
          tiger.

                    MAGDA
          Angel. Not tiger. Angel.

                    JES
          (rolling his eyes) Yeah, right.
          Aw... I'm so excited we can take
          him to Turin for the exhibit. I
          know he won't remember it but --

                    MAGDA
          You never know...the Shroud sure
          had a big impact on you. (beat) So
          what are you going to call your
          blog?

                    JES
That's what I'm a little stuck on.
The Shroud exhibit is called:
"PASSIO CHRISTI, PASSIO HOMINIS"
which means Passion of Christ,
Passion of Men. The blog will be
centered on the topic of
reconciling human suffering.
(shaking his head) But if I call it
"Passion of Men" search engines
would probably link it to a bunch
of gay porn sites. (they laugh)

                    MAGDA
Huh...it's tricky; you have to find
just the right name.

                    JES
Yeah. I also want the name to be
closely tied to the Sindone, since
I want to blog about it too --
especially after the exhibition. I
keep thinking about what Cardinal
Cavelli said to me -- that he
believes the Shroud is a "Divine
Remedy" that Christ left for us. He
likened it to a going away present.
(beat) What do you think of
divineremedy.org?

                    MAGDA
I think it's absolutely perfect.
(beat) So, I'll be living with a
daily blogger guy, eh?

                    JES
Don't know about daily. We'll see
what comes down the inspiration
pike.

                    MAGDA
(looking at the computer monitor)
Will you read it to me?

                    JES
(reluctantly) I don't know...it's
just a draft of my first post.
Plus, you're the writer in the
family.

                    MAGDA
          (sitting in his lap, cooing softly)
          Pretty please read me a bedtime
          story...

                    JES
          Okay...but go easy on me. So...my
          thinking is, if people want to
          reconcile their suffering, they
          have to first really examine
          suffering honestly. No sugar
          coating it.

                    MAGDA
          Agreed. Now read already.

Jes encloses her in his arms and begins READING ALOUD.

                    JES
          Recipe for Reconciling Human
          Suffering: Chapter 1: Honest
          Identification of the Problem.

CONTINUOUS:

MONTAGE: Images overlap onto the screen in SILENCE and slow motion to the (VOICE OVER) of Jes READING ALOUD.

-- A WAR VETERAN sits at a bar drinking shots of whiskey while having flashbacks of fighter jets making streaks across the sky above MEN who are fighting and dying during combat on a barren, bloody battlefield.

                    JES (VOICE OVER)
          It's the only constant...
          We can count on it, in any number
          of forms throughout our individual
          and the human life span. It is 100
          percent guaranteed, though the
          degree, severity, impact and
          repercussions will vary. It is non-
          negotiable, out of our control, as
          certain as death and taxes.

-- A WOMAN gives birth to a healthy BABY in a hospital. A COUPLE happily exchange wedding vows on the beach. A MARCHING BAND parades down a small town street.

                    JES
          It is interrupted by short-lived
          periods of joy, moments of grace,
          and soft reprieves that make it
          barely tolerable.

-- A starving FAMILY wanders through a burned down village in Darfur. A wealthy CELEBRITY lounges by the pool at her Beverly Hills mansion.

                      JES
           It can always be held to
           comparisons of worse or better
           variations.

-- SHOPPERS in Paris pass a HOMELESS MAN on the street, avoiding making eye contact with him. PATIENTS in a cancer clinic are receiving chemotherapy.

                      JES
           It binds us to guilt for what we
           have, to fear of what we might
           lose.

-- A WOMAN admires engagement rings in a jewelry shop window. A lonely, elderly WIDOWER stares at a photo of his beloved, late wife.

                      JES
           It intoxicates us with hope of
           what's to come and cripples us with
           envy of others for what we lack.

-- A TEENAGE GIRL reads a pamphlet from an abortion clinic, agonizing about what to do. A middle-aged MAN holds a razor blade to his wrist and closes his eyes.

                      JES
           It meddles with the mind, leaving
           little or no room for peace. It
           toys with the emotions, exposing us
           to layers upon layers of
           vulnerability.

-- A STREET GANG watches as one member shoots an innocent PEDESTRIAN as part of an initiation ceremony. TERRORISTS train at a camp up in the mountains of Afghanistan.

                      JES
           It unleashes the poisons of
           paranoia and anger by feasting on
           steady frustration and bitter
           disappointment.

-- A MAN on death row stands behind prison bars, holding a Bible and crying. A FAMILY agonizes over a LOVED ONE who is lying in a hospital bed in a coma on life support machines.

JES
It simultaneously fosters and
annihilates faith.

-- The film stops abruptly then begins to replay all of the
images just seen in reverse and at a very fast speed.

JES
It rises with the sun and crawls
deep into the day's length until
night descends and it curls up in
bed with us to taunt our dreams.
It is the ultimate trap and our
only salvation because accepting
it, escaping it, neutralizing it,
loving it, transcending it,
releasing it, embracing it all lead
to one reality...

-- The images blur and The HOLY FACE OF THE SHROUD OF TURIN
appears and undulates in slow motion across the screen.

JES
That it is the only constant...(his
VOICE FADES into SILENCE)

FADE TO BLACK.

TITLE: www.divineremedy.org

www.ingramcontent.com/pod-product-compliance
Lightning Source LLC
Chambersburg PA
CBHW080557090426
42735CB00016B/3263